LET'S PRAISE!

WORDS EDITION

Editor: David Peacock

Consultant: Graham Kendrick

Executive Editor: Michael Perry

Marshall Pickering

Marshall Morgan & Scott
Marshall Pickering
34–42 Cleveland Street, London W1P 5FB

Copyright details will be found with each item, and further information at the page 'Legal Information'. Every effort as been made to trace copyright holders and obtain permission; the publishers would welcome details of any error or omission, which will be corrected in future reprints.

First published in 1988 by Marshall Morgan & Scott Publications Ltd., part of the Marshall Pickering Holdings Group.

Reprinted : Impression number
89 90 91   : 10 9 8 7 6 5 4 3 2

British Library Cataloguing in Publication Data
Let's Praise – Words Edition
    1. Hymns, English
    I. Peacock, David

    ISBN 0-551-01696-5

Text set by Barnes Music Engraving Ltd, East Sussex.
Printed in Great Britain by The Bath Press, Avon.

PREFACE TO LET'S PRAISE!

We have researched the songs young people are singing across the denominations and throughout the world, and we believe the result to be a magnificent collection of material, suitable for all occasions involving young people.

Styles and Sources

Let's Praise! songs range from soft to hard rock, from reggae to black gospel; from performance items to recently composed and previously unpublished material; from jazz to response-style psalms and hymns.

A good selection of music from Africa can be found in the book alongside material from, for example, Scandinavia, Germany, and South America. Previously unpublished rock worship songs from Australia are included in the collection. Taizé music, which has long been popular amongst thousands of European young people, is well represented.

All this, together with most of the popular and current worship songs from Britain and North America, make *Let's Praise!* a truly distinctive songbook for young people. All the Graham Kendrick *Make Way 1 – A Carnival of Praise* street procession songs are in the book (in march order) together with a good selection of songs from *Make Way 2 – Shine, Jesus, Shine.*

We believe that there is tremendous value in having hymns of deep spiritual content, which are also in a language understandable to today's generation, included in the *Let's Praise!* collection. This results in a songbook readily available for use in youth groups, colleges and universities, youth houseparties and conferences. It is the ideal songbook for youth services in churches – even as your church's basic songbook.

The extensive indexes will help you use *Let's Praise!* to the best possible advantage. Also available in the music edition are: Foreword, Finding your way around, Notes about the music (with chord chart), Index to authors and originators of texts, Index to composers, arrangers and sources of music, Index to themes, Index to musical styles, Index to hymns (with tunes), Index to vocal arrangements, Index to instrumental arrangements.

We commend this songbook to the new generation of Christians around the world, praying it will enrich our worship and give expression to our concern for sharing the Christian gospel with a world in need.

David Peacock

1

Dave Bilbrough
© 1977 Thankyou Music

Abba, Father, let me be
   yours and yours alone;
may my will for ever be,
   evermore your own.
Never let my heart grow cold,
   never let me go:
Abba, Father, let me be
   yours and yours alone!

2

After E Perronet (1725–1792)
and J Rippon (1751–1836)
© in this version Jubilate Hymns †

1 All hail the power of Jesus' name!
  let kings before him fall,
  his power and majesty proclaim
  and crown him, crown him, crown him,
  crown him Lord of all.

2 Come, crown him, moon and stars of night;
  he made you, great and small:
  bright sun, praise him who gave you light
  and crown him . . .

3 Crown him, you martyrs spurning pain,
  who witnessed to his call;
  now sing your victory-song again
  and crown him . . .

4 Let all who trust in Christ exclaim
  in wonder, to recall
  the one who bore our sin and shame,
  and crown him . . .

5 Then in that final judgement hour
  when all rebellions fall,
  we'll rise in his triumphant power
  and crown him . . .

2A

PRAISE SHOUT
From Psalm 104

LEADER Praise the Lord, O my soul;
ALL   **praise the Lord!**

LEADER O Lord my God, how great you are;
ALL   **robed in majesty and splendour.**

LEADER Praise the Lord, O my soul;
ALL   **praise the Lord! Amen.**

3

After Christer Hultgren
Jeanne Harper
© 1978 Förlaget Filadelfia Dagenhuset

1 All I am will sing out as a praise song –
  every note, every tone is for you;
  whether days will be hard or be easy,
  I will live every moment for you.
    You have all of the praise I can offer,
    for your love is to one who has no merit:
    here I am, take me Lord, and my worship,
    for your goodness and grace have no limit.

2 There is nobody else who is worthy –
  to nobody else can I sing;
  and to you will be all of the glory
  in heaven where my praises I'll bring.
    You have . . .

3 If at times through my silence I grieve you,
  if through doubt, praise and worshipping cease;
  then, Lord, open my eyes that I see you,
  see in you alone I have peace.
    You have . . .

4

Shimrit Orr and Kobi Oshrat
© 1979 Gogly Music /
International Music Publications

Alleluia, praise the Lord,
Alleluia, in one accord!
When it seems there are no words to say
all the love I get from the Lord today,
when my heart sings out with joy – Alleluia.
Alleluia, is my song,
alleluia the whole day long,
alleluia, the heavens are ringing
with everyone singing 'Alleluia!'

Alleluia, praise the Lord . . .

Alleluia, the heavens are ringing
with everyone singing 'Alleluia!'

5

African origin edited by Anders Nyberg
© Wild Goose Publications / The Iona Community

Alleluia!
We sing your praises,
all our hearts
are filled with gladness.
Alleluia . . .

1 Christ the Lord to us said,
  'I am wine, I am bread';
  'I am wine, I am bread' –
  give to all who thirst and hunger.
  Alleluia . . .

2 Now he sends us all out,
  strong in faith, free of doubt;
  strong in faith, free of doubt –
  tell the earth the joyful Gospel.
  Alleluia . . .

AFRICAN VERSES
*Haleluya! Pelo tsa rona,
di thabile kaofela.
Haleluya . . .*

1 *Ke Morena Jeso,
ya re dumeletseng,
ya re dumeletseng,
ho tsamaisa evangedi.
Haleluya . . .*

2 *O na na le bo mang?
Le barutuwa ba hae:
O na na le bo mang?
Lo baruluwa ba hae.
Haleluya . . .*

6

J Newton (1725–1807)
© in this version Jubilate Hymns †

1 Amazing grace – how sweet the sound –
that saved a wretch like me!
I once was lost, but now am found;
was blind, but now I see.

2 God's grace first taught my heart to fear,
his grace my fears relieved:
how precious did that grace appear
the hour I first believed!

3 Through every danger, trial and snare
I have already come;
for grace has brought me safe thus far,
and grace will lead me home.

4 The Lord has promised good to me,
his word my hope secures;
my shield and stronghold he shall be
as long as life endures.

5 And when this earthly life is past,
and mortal cares shall cease,
I shall possess with Christ at last
eternal joy and peace.

7

From The Alternative Service Book 1980
© 1980 Central Board of Finance of the Church of England

Almighty God, our heavenly Father,
we have sinned against you,
and against our fellow men,

in thought and word and deed,
through negligence, through weakness,
through our own deliberate fault.

We are truly sorry
and repent of all our sins.
For the sake of your Son, Jesus Christ,
who died for us,
who died for us,
who died for us,

forgive us all that is past;
and grant that we may serve you
in newness of life
MEN   to the glory of your name,
WOMEN to the glory of your name,
MEN   to the glory of your name,
WOMEN to the glory of your name,
ALL   to the glory of your name.

Amen, amen.

8

C Wesley (1707–1788)

1 And can it be that I should gain
an interest in the Saviour's blood?
Died he for me, who caused his pain;
for me, who him to death pursued?
Amazing love! – how can it be
that you, my God, should die for me?

2 What mystery here! – the Immortal dies;
who can explore his strange design?
In vain the first-born seraph tries
to sound the depths of love divine.
Such mercy this! – let earth adore;
let angel minds enquire no more.

3 He left his Father's throne above –
so free, so infinite his grace –
emptied himself of all but love,
and bled for Adam's helpless race.
What mercy this, immense and free,
for, O my God, it found out me!

4 Long my imprisoned spirit lay,
fast bound in sin and nature's night:
your sunrise turned that night to day;
I woke – the dungeon flamed with light.
My chains fell off, my heart was free;
I rose, went out to liberty!

5 No condemnation now I dread;
Jesus, and all in him, is mine!
Alive in him, my living head,
and clothed in righteousness divine,
bold I approach the eternal throne
and claim the crown through Christ my own.

9

C M Noel (1817–1877)
© in this version Jubilate Hymns †

1 At the name of Jesus
every knee shall bow,
every tongue confess him
king of glory now;
this the Father's pleasure,
that we call him Lord,
who from the beginning
was the mighty word.

2 At his voice creation
sprang at once to sight,
all the angel faces,
all the hosts of light;
thrones and dominations,
stars upon their way,
all the heavenly orders,
in their great array.

3 Humbled for a season,
to receive a name
from the lips of sinners
unto whom he came;
faithfully he bore it
spotless to the last,
brought it back victorious
when from death he passed:

4 Bore it up triumphant
with its human light,
through all ranks of creatures
to the central height;
to the eternal Godhead,
to the Father's throne,
filled it to the glory
of his triumph won.

5 Name him, Christians, name him,
    with love strong as death,
but with awe and wonder,
    and with bated breath:
he is God the saviour,
    he is Christ the Lord,
ever to be worshipped,
    trusted and adored.

6 In your hearts enthrone him –
    there let him subdue
all that is not holy,
    all that is not true;
crown him as your captain
    in temptation's hour,
let his will enfold you
    in its light and power.

7 With his Father's glory
    Jesus comes again,
angel hosts attend him
    and announce his reign;
for all wreaths of empire
    meet upon his brow,
and our hearts confess him
    king of glory now.

10 From Revelation 1
Dave Fellingham
© 1982 Thankyou Music

1 At your feet we fall,
    mighty risen Lord,
as we come before your throne
    to worship you!
By your Spirit's power
    you now draw our hearts,
and we hear your voice
    in triumph ringing clear:
    'I am he that lives,
    that lives and was dead:
    behold I am alive –
    alive evermore!'

2 There we see you stand,
    mighty risen Lord,
clothed in garments pure and holy,
    shining bright;
eyes of flashing fire,
    feet like burnished bronze,
and the sound of many waters
    is your voice.
    'I am he that lives . . .

3 Like the shining sun
    in its noon-day strength,
we now see the glory
    of your wondrous face:
once that face was marred,
    but now you're glorified;
and your words, like a two-edged sword,
    have mighty power.
    'I am he that lives . . .

11 Morris Chapman
© 1983 Word Music (UK)

Be bold, be strong,
for the Lord your God is with you;
be bold, be strong,
for the Lord your God is with you!
    I am not afraid,
    I am not dismayed,
because I'm walking in faith and victory:
come on and walk in faith and victory,
for the Lord your God is with you!

12 Bob Gillman
© 1977 Thankyou Music,

Bind us together, Lord,
bind us together
with cords that cannot be broken;
bind us together, Lord,
bind us together,
O bind us together in love!

1 There is only one God,
there is only one King,
there is only one Body –
that is why we sing:
    Bind us together . . .

2 We are the family of God,
joined by the Spirit above,
working together with Christ,
growing and building in love.
    Bind us together . . .

13 David Evans
© 1986 Thankyou Music

1 Be still,
for the presence of the Lord,
    the holy One, is here;
come bow before him now
with reverence and fear:
in him no sin is found –
we stand on holy ground.
Be still,
for the presence of the Lord,
    the holy One, is here.

2 Be still,
for the glory of the Lord
    is shining all around;
he burns with holy fire,
with splendour he is crowned:
how awesome is the sight –
our radiant king of light!
Be still,
for the glory of the Lord
    is shining all around.

3 Be still,
for the power of the Lord
   is moving in this place:
he comes to cleanse and heal,
to minister his grace –
no work too hard for him.
In faith receive from him.
Be still,
for the power of the Lord
   is moving in this place.

14
From Psalm 103
Unknown

Bless the Lord, O my soul,
bless the Lord, O my soul,
and all that is within me
bless his holy name;
bless the Lord . . .
   King of kings (for ever and ever),
   Lord of lords (for ever and ever)
   King of kings (for ever and ever),
   King of kings and Lord of lords!

Bless the Lord . . .

15
Derived from the 'Daily Office'
© Joint Liturgical Group

SOLO/GROUP
Bless the Lord the God of our fathers:
ALL
sing his praise and exalt him for ever.

SOLO/GROUP
Bless his holy and glorious name:
ALL
sing his praise and exalt him for ever.

SOLO/GROUP
Bless him in his holy and glorious temple:
ALL
sing his praise and exalt him for ever.

SOLO/GROUP
Bless him who beholds the depths:
ALL
sing his praise and exalt him for ever.

SOLO/GROUP
Bless him who sits between the cherubim:
ALL
sing his praise and exalt him for ever.

SOLO/GROUP
Bless him on the throne of his kingdom:
ALL
sing his praise and exalt him for ever.

SOLO/GROUP
Bless him in the heights of heaven:
ALL
sing his praise and exalt him for ever.

SOLO/GROUP
Bless the Father, the Son and Holy Spirit:
ALL
sing his praise and exalt him for ever.

16
E Hatch (1835–1889)
© in this version Jubilate Hymns †

1 Breathe on me, breath of God:
fill me with life anew,
that as you love, so I may love,
and do what you would do.

2 Breathe on me, breath of God,
until my heart is pure,
until my will is one with yours
to do and to endure.

3 Breathe on me, breath of God;
fulfil my heart's desire,
until this earthly part of me
glows with your heavenly fire.

4 Breathe on me, breath of God:
so shall I never die,
but live with you the perfect life
of your eternity.

17
From Psalms 149 and 150
© Michael Perry / Jubilate Hymns †

1 Bring to the Lord a glad new song,
children of grace, extol your king;
worship and praise to God belong –
to instruments of music, sing!
Let those be warned who spurn his name;
nations and kings, attend his word –
God's justice shall bring tyrants shame:
let every creature praise the Lord!

2 Praise him within these hallowed walls,
praise him beneath the dome of heaven;
by cymbals' sounds and trumpets' calls
let praises fit for God be given:
with strings and brass and wind rejoice –
then, join his praise with full accord
all living things with breath and voice:
let every creature praise the Lord!

18
Janet Lunt
© 1978 Mustard Seed Music

Broken for me, broken for you,
the body of Jesus broken for you.

1 He offered his body, he poured out his soul,
Jesus was broken that we might be whole:
   Broken for me . . .

2 Come to my table and with me dine,
eat of my bread and drink of my wine:
   Broken for me . . .

3 This is my body given for you,
eat it remembering I died for you:
   Broken for me . . .

4 This is my blood I shed for you,
for your forgiveness, making you new:
   Broken for me . . .

19

H B George (1838–1910)

1 By every nation, race and tongue,
worship and praise be ever sung;
    praise the Father: Alleluia!
For pardoned sin, death overcome,
and hopes that live beyond the tomb:
    Alleluia, alleluia;
    alleluia, alleluia, alleluia!

2 Saints who on earth have suffered long,
for Jesus' sake enduring wrong,
    ever faithful: Alleluia!
Where faith is lost in sight, rejoice
and sing with never-wearied voice:
    Alleluia . . .

3 Let earth and air and sea unite
to celebrate his glorious might,
    their creator: Alleluia!
Sun, moon and stars in endless space
echo the song of every race:
    Alleluia . . .

20

Eddie Espinosa
© 1982 Mercy Publishing / Thankyou Music

Change my heart, O God,
make it ever true;
change my heart, O God,
may I be like you.
You are the potter, I am the clay;
mould me and make me,
this is what I pray.

Change my heart . . .

Change my heart, O God,
make it ever true.
Change my heart, O God,
may I be like you.

21

© Michael Saward / Jubilate Hymns †

1 Christ triumphant, ever reigning,
Saviour, Master, King!
Lord of heaven, our lives sustaining,
hear us as we sing:
    Yours the glory and the crown,
    the high renown,
        the eternal name.

2 Word incarnate, truth revealing,
Son of Man on earth!
power and majesty concealing
by your humble birth:
    Yours the glory . . .

3 Suffering servant, scorned, ill-treated,
victim crucified!
death is through the cross defeated,
sinners justified:
    Yours the glory . . .

4 Priestly king, enthroned for ever
high in heaven above!
sin and death and hell shall never
stifle hymns of love:
    Yours the glory . . .

5 So, our hearts and voices raising
through the ages long,
ceaselessly upon you gazing,
this shall be our song:
    Yours the glory . . .

22

Graham Kendrick
© 1988 Make Way Music / Thankyou Music

1 MEN Clear the road, make wide the way;
WOMEN clear the road, make wide the way!
MEN Welcome now the God who saves;
WOMEN welcome now the God who saves!
MEN Fill the streets with shouts of joy;
WOMEN fill the streets with shouts of joy!
MEN   Prepare the way of the Lord,
WOMEN   prepare the way of the Lord;
MEN   prepare the way
ALL   of the Lord!

2 MEN Raise your voice and join the song,
WOMEN raise your voice and join the song:
MEN God made flesh to us has come,
WOMEN God made flesh to us has come.
MEN Welcome him, your banners wave;
WOMEN welcome him, your banners wave!
MEN   Prepare the way of the Lord . . .

3 MEN For all sin the price is paid,
WOMEN for all sin the price is paid.
MEN All our sins on Jesus laid,
WOMEN all our sins on Jesus laid.
MEN By his blood we are made clean;
WOMEN by his blood we are made clean.
MEN   Prepare the way of the Lord . . .

4 MEN At his feet, come, humbly bow,
WOMEN at his feet, come, humbly bow.
MEN In your lives enthrone him now,
WOMEN in your lives enthrone him now.
MEN See, your great Deliverer comes;
WOMEN see, your great Deliverer comes!
MEN   Prepare the way of the Lord . . .

23

© Bernadette Farrell /
Magnificat Music

Come to set us free,
come to make us your own;
come to show the way
to your people, your chosen:
open our lives to the light of your promise.
Come to our hearts with healing,
come to our minds with power;
come to us and bring us your life.

1 You are light which shines in darkness,
Morning Star which never sets:
open our eyes which only dimly see
the truth which sets us free.
    Come to set us free . . .

2 You are hope which brings us courage,
   you are strength which never fails:
   open our minds to ways we do not know,
   but where your Spirit grows.
       Come to set us free . . .

3 You are promise of salvation,
   you are God in human form:
   bring to our world of emptiness and fear
   the word we long to hear.
       Come to set us free . . .

24 From Psalm 95
Brent Chambers
© 1985 Scripture in Song / Thankyou Music

Come, let us sing for joy to the Lord,
come, let us sing for joy to the Lord,
come, let us sing for joy to the Lord,
come, let us sing for joy to the Lord!

   Come, let us sing for joy to the Lord,
   let us shout aloud
   to the Rock of our salvation;
   come, let us sing . . .

1 Let us come before him with thanksgiving,
   and extol him with music and song:
   for the Lord, our Lord, is the great God,
   the great king above all gods.
       Come, let us sing for joy to the Lord,
       let us shout aloud . . .

2 Let us bow before him in our worship,
   let us kneel before God, our great king;
   for he is our God, and we are his people –
   that's why we shout and sing!
       Come, let us sing for joy to the Lord,
       let us shout aloud . . .

25 Patricia Morgan
© 1984 Thankyou Music

Come on and celebrate!
His gift of love we will celebrate –
the Son of God, who loved us
and gave us life:
We'll shout your praise, O King:
you give us joy nothing else can bring;
we'll give to you our offering
in celebration praise.

   Come on and celebrate, celebrate,
   celebrate and sing,
   celebrate and sing to the King:
   Come on and celebrate, celebrate,
   celebrate and sing,
   celebrate and sing to the King!

26 M Bridges (1800–1894)
and G Thring (1823–1903)
© in this version Word & Music / Jubilate Hymns †

1 Crown him with many crowns,
   the Lamb upon his throne,
   while heaven's eternal anthem drowns
   all music but its own!

Awake my soul, and sing
of him who died to be
your saviour and your matchless king
through all eternity.

2 Crown him the Lord of life
   triumphant from the grave,
   who rose victorious from the strife
   for those he came to save:
   his glories now we sing
   who died and reigns on high;
   who died eternal life to bring
   and lives that death may die.

3 Crown him the Lord of love,
   who shows his hands and side –
   those wounds yet visible above
   in beauty glorified.
   No angel in the sky
   can fully bear that sight,
   but downward bends his burning eye
   at mysteries so bright.

4 Crown him the Lord of years,
   the potentate of time,
   creator of the rolling spheres
   in majesty sublime:
   all hail Redeemer, hail,
   for you have died for me;
   your praise shall never, never fail
   through all eternity!

27 Graham Kendrick
© 1985 Thankyou Music

1 Darkness like a shroud
   covers the earth,
   evil like a cloud
   covers the people;
   but the Lord will rise upon you,
   and his glory will appear on you,
   nations will come to your light.
       Arise, shine, your light has come,
       the glory of the Lord has risen on you;
       arise, shine, your light has come –
       Jesus the light of the world has come.

2 Children of the light,
   be clean and pure;
   rise, you sleepers,
   Christ will shine on you:
   take the Spirit's flashing two-edged sword
   and with faith declare God's mighty word;
   stand up, and in his strength be strong!
       Arise, shine . . .

3 Here among us now,
   Christ the Light
   kindles brighter flames
   in our trembling hearts:
   Living Word, our lamp, come guide our feet –
   as we walk as one in light and peace,
   justice and truth shine like the sun.
       Arise, shine . . .

4 Like a city bright,
so let us blaze;
lights in every street
turning night to day:
and the darkness shall not overcome,
till the fullness of Christ's kingdom comes,
dawning to God's eternal day.

   Arise, shine, your light has come,
   the glory of the Lord has risen on you;
   arise, shine, your light has come –
Jesus the light of the world,
Jesus the light of the world,
Jesus the light of the world has come.

28
Michael W Smith
© 1983 Meadowgreen Music / Tree Publishing Co

Emmanuel, Emmanuel,
Wonderful counsellor,
Lord of life, Lord of all –
he's the Prince of peace,
mighty God, holy One,
Emmanuel, Emmanuel,

Emmanuel . . .

29
From the Alternative Service Book 1980
© The Central Board of Finance
of the Church of England

Eternal God and Father,
eternal God and Father,
eternal God and Father,
eternal God and Father:

You create us by your power
and redeem us by your love:
guide and strengthen us by your Spirit,
that we may give ourselves
   in love and service
to one another and to you;
   Eternal God and Father . . .

through Jesus Christ our Lord.
Amen, amen.

30
Ian Smale
© 1984 Thankyou Music

Father God, I wonder
how I managed to exist
without the knowledge
of your parenthood
and your loving care.
But now I am your child,
I am adopted in your family,
and I can never be alone
because, Father God,
you're there beside me.
   I will sing your praises,
   I will sing your praises,
   I will sing your praises for evermore;
   I will sing your praises,
   I will sing your praises,
   I will sing your praises for evermore.

31
Dave Bilbrough
© 1985 Thankyou Music

1 Father in heaven,
our voices we raise:
receive our devotion,
receive now our praise
as we sing of the glory
of all that you've done –
the greatest love-story
that's ever been sung.
   And we will crown you Lord of all,
   yes, we will crown you Lord of all,
   for you have won the victory:
   yes, we will crown you Lord of all.

2 Father, in heaven,
our lives are your own;
we've been caught by a vision
of Jesus alone –
who came as a servant
to free us from sin:
Father in heaven,
our worship we bring.
   And we will crown . . .

3 We will sing Alleluia,
we will sing to the King,
to our mighty deliverer
our alleluias will ring.
Yes, our praise is resounding
to the Lamb on the throne:
he alone is exalted
through the love he has shown.
   And we will crown . . .

32
Bob Fitts
© 1985 Scripture in Song / Thankyou Music

Father in heaven, how we love you:
we lift your name in all the earth.
May your kingdom
      be established in our praises
as your people declare your mighty works.

Blessed be the Lord God almighty
who was and is and is to come:
blessed be the Lord God almighty
who reigns for evermore!

33
From The Lord's Prayer
J E Seddon (1915–1983)
© Mrs M Seddon / Jubilate Hymns †

1 Father God in heaven,
      Lord most high:
hear your children's prayer,
      Lord most high:
hallowed be your name,
      Lord most high –
O Lord, hear our prayer.

2 May your kingdom come
      here on earth;
   may your will be done
      here on earth,
   as it is in heaven
      so on earth –
      O Lord, hear our prayer.

3 Give us daily bread
      day by day,
   and forgive our sins
      day by day,
   as we too forgive
      day by day –
      O Lord, hear our prayer.

4 Lead us in your way,
      make us strong;
   when temptations come
      make us strong;
   save us all from sin,
      keep us strong –
      O Lord, hear our prayer.

5 All things come from you,
      all are yours –
   kingdom, glory, power,
      all are yours;
   take our lives and gifts,
      all are yours –
      O Lord, hear our prayer.

34
Terry Coelho
© 1972 Maranatha! Music / Word Music (UK)

1 Father, we adore you,
   lay our lives before you:
   how we love you!

2 Jesus, we adore you,
   lay our lives before you:
   how we love you!

3 Spirit, we adore you,
   lay our lives before you:
   how we love you!

34A   PRAISE SHOUT
From Psalm 92

LEADER It is good to praise you, Lord,
ALL   **and make music to your name:**

LEADER To proclaim your constant love in the
            morning,
ALL   **and tell your faithfulness in the evening**

LEADER For you, O Lord, are exalted for ever.
ALL   **Amen.**

35
© 1987 Phil Pringle / Thankyou Music

   'Fear not, for I am with you,
   fear not, for I am with you,
   fear not, for I am with you!'
   says the Lord.
   'Fear not . . .

'I have redeemed you,
I have called you by name –
child, you are mine:
when you walk through the waters
      I'll be there;
and through the flame,
you'll not (no way!) be drowned,
you'll not (no way!) be burned,
   for I am with you.'
   'Fear not . . .

36
From Psalm 24
Graham Kendrick
© 1988 Make Way Music / Thankyou Music

1 ALL   Fling wide your doors, O you streets,
             open up you hearts of men,
             that the King of glory may come in;
             fling wide your doors, O you streets,
             open up you hearts of men,
             that the King of glory may come in!

   WOMEN Who is this King of glory?
   MEN   The Lord, strong and mighty.
   WOMEN Who is this King, this King of glory?
   MEN   The Lord – his name is Jesus!

2 ALL   Fling wide your doors . . .

3 ALL   Fling wide your doors . . .

   LEADER Fling wide your doors,
   ALL   fling wide your doors,
   LEADER O you streets,
   ALL   O you streets –
             open up you hearts of men!
   LEADER Fling wide your doors,
   ALL   fling wide your doors,
   LEADER O you streets,
   ALL   O you streets –
             open up you hearts of men!

37
Dave Richards
© 1977 Thankyou Music

   For I'm building a people of power –
   and I'm making a people of praise,
   that will move through this land by my Spirit,
   and will glorify my holy name.

   Build your Church, Lord; make us strong, Lord,
   join our hearts, Lord, through your Son;
   make us one, Lord, in your Body,
   in the kingdom of your Son!

38
© 1969, 1987 James Quinn S.J.
reprinted by permission of Geoffrey Chapman /
Cassell Publishers Ltd

1 Forth in the peace of Christ we go,
   Christ to the world with joy we bring;
   Christ in our minds, Christ on our lips,
   Christ in our hearts, the world's true king.

2 King of our hearts, Christ makes us kings –
   kingship with him his servants gain;
   with Christ, the Servant-Lord of all,
   Christ's world we serve to share Christ's reign.

3 Priests of the world, Christ sends us forth
the world of time to consecrate,
our world of sin by grace to heal,
Christ's world in Christ to re-create.

4 Prophets of Christ, we hear his word:
he claims our minds, to search his ways,
he claims our lips, to speak his truth,
he claims our hearts, to sing his praise.

5 We are his church; he makes us one:
here is one hearth for all to find,
here is one flock, one Shepherd-King,
here is one faith, one heart, one mind.

39
Graham Kendrick
© 1985 Thankyou Music

1 For this purpose Christ was revealed,
to destroy all the works of the evil one;
Christ in us has overcome,
so with gladness we sing
and welcome his kingdom in.
> MEN   Over sin he has conquered:
> WOMEN   Alleluia! he has conquered.
> MEN   Over death victorious:
> WOMEN   Alleluia! victorious.
> MEN   Over sickness he has triumphed:
> WOMEN   Alleluia! he has triumphed.
> ALL   Jesus reigns over all!

2 In the name of Jesus we stand;
by the power of his blood
we now claim this ground:
Satan has no authority here,
powers of darkness must flee,
for Christ has the victory.
> MEN   Over sin . . .

40
Graham Kendrick
© 1983 Thankyou Music

1 From heaven you came, helpless Babe –
entered our world your glory veiled,
not to be served but to serve,
and give your life that we might live.
> This is our God – the servant king,
> he calls us now to follow him,
> to bring our lives as a daily offering
> of worship to the servant king.

2 There in the garden of tears
my heavy load he chose to bear;
his heart with sorrow was torn,
'Yet not my will but yours,' he said.
> This is our God . . .

3 Come see his hands and his feet,
the scars that speak of sacrifice,
hands that flung stars into space
to cruel nails surrendered.
> This is our God . . .

4 So let us learn how to serve
and in our lives enthrone him,
each other's needs to prefer –
for it is Christ we are serving,
> This is our God . . .

41
Graham Kendrick
© 1988 Make Way Music / Thankyou Music

1 From the sun's rising
     unto the sun's setting
Jesus our Lord
     shall be great in the earth;
and all earth's kingdom
     shall be his dominion –
all of creation
     shall sing of his worth.
> Let every heart, every voice,
> every tongue join with spirits ablaze:
> one in his love
> we will circle the world
> with the song of his praise.
> O let all his people rejoice,
> and let all the earth hear his voice!

2 To every tongue, tribe
     and nation he sends us,
to make disciples,
     to teach and baptize;
for all authority
     to him is given –
now as his witnesses
     we shall arise.
> Let every heart . . .

3 Come let us join with
     the church from all nations,
cross every border,
     throw wide every door:
workers with him
     as he gathers his harvest,
till earth's far corners
     our saviour adore.
> Let every heart . . .

> Let all his people rejoice,
> and let all the earth hear his voice!

42
Henry Smith
© 1978 Hosanna! Music / Frontier Music

> Give thanks with a grateful heart,
> give thanks to the Holy One;
> give thanks because he's given
> Jesus Christ, his Son.
> Give thanks . . .

> And now let the weak say 'I am strong',
> let the poor say 'I am rich',
> because of what the Lord has done for us;
> and now let the weak say 'I am strong',
> let the poor say 'I am rich',
> because of what the Lord has done for us.
> Give thanks . . .

> And now . . .

43
From *Gloria in excelsis*
© Christopher Idle / Jubilate Hymns †

1 Glory in the highest
   to the God of heaven!
Peace to all your people
   through the earth be given!
Mighty God and Father,
   thanks and praise we bring,
singing Alleluia
   to our heavenly king;
singing Alleluia
   to our heavenly king.

2 Jesus Christ is risen,
   God the Father's Son!
With the Holy Spirit,
   you are Lord alone!
Lamb once killed for sinners,
   all our guilt to bear,
show us now your mercy,
   now receive our prayer;
show us now your mercy,
   now receive our prayer.

3 Christ the world's true Saviour,
   high and holy one,
seated now and reigning
   from your Father's throne:
Lord and God, we praise you!
   Highest heaven adores:
in the Father's glory,
   all the praise be yours;
in the Father's glory,
   all the praise be yours!

44
From Revelation 4 and 5
derived from the 'Daily Office'
© Joint Liturgical Group

Glory and honour and power
are yours by right, O Lord our God;
for you created all things,
and by your will they have their being.

Glory and honour and power
are yours by right, O Lamb who was slain;
for by your blood you ransomed us for God:
   from every race and language,
   from every people and nation:
   to make us a kingdom of priests
   to stand and serve before our God.

To him who sits on the throne and to the Lamb,
be praise and honour, glory and might,
for ever and ever and ever. Amen, amen.

45
From *Te Deum*
© Christopher Idle / Jubilate Hymns †

1 God, we praise you! God, we bless you!
God, we name you sovereign Lord!
Mighty king whom angels worship,
Father, by your church adored:
all creation shows your glory,
heaven and earth draw near your throne
singing 'Holy, holy, holy,'
Lord of hosts, and God alone!

2 True apostles, faithful prophets,
saints who set their world ablaze,
martyrs, once unknown, unheeded,
join one growing song of praise,
while your church on earth confesses
one majestic Trinity:
Father, Son, and Holy Spirit,
God, our hope eternally.

3 Jesus Christ, the king of glory
everlasting Son of God,
humble was your virgin mother,
hard the lonely path you trod:
by your cross is sin defeated,
hell confronted face to face,
heaven opened to believers,
sinners justified by grace.

4 Christ, at God's right hand victorious,
you will judge the world you made;
Lord, in mercy help your servants
for whose freedom you have paid:
raise us up from dust to glory,
guard us from all sin today;
King enthroned above all praises,
save your people, God, we pray.

46
J E Seddon (1915–1983)
© Mrs M Seddon / Jubilate Hymns †

1 Go forth and tell!
   O church of God, awake!
God's saving news
   to all the nations take:
proclaim Christ Jesus,
   saviour, Lord, and king,
that all the world
   his worthy praise may sing.

2 Go forth and tell!
   God's love embraces all;
he will in grace
   respond to all who call:
how shall they call
   if they have never heard
the gracious invitation
   of his word?

3 Go forth and tell!
   where still the darkness lies;
in wealth or want,
   the sinner surely dies:
give us, O Lord,
   concern of heart and mind,
a love like yours
   which cares for humankind.

4 Go forth and tell!
   The doors are open wide:
share God's good gifts –
   let no one be denied;
live out your life
   as Christ your Lord shall choose,
your ransomed powers
   for his sole glory use.

5 Go forth and tell!
    O church of God, arise!
go in the strength
    which Christ your Lord supplies;
go till all nations
    his great name adore
and serve him, Lord and king
    for evermore.

47 From Psalm 46
© Richard Bewes / Jubilate Hymns †

1 God is our strength and refuge,
our present help in trouble;
and we therefore will not fear,
though the earth should change!
Though mountains shake and tremble,
though swirling floods are raging,
God the Lord of hosts is with us evermore!

2 There is a flowing river,
within God's holy city;
God is in the midst of her –
she shall not be moved!
God's help is swiftly given,
thrones vanish at his presence –
God the Lord of hosts is with us evermore!

3 Come, see the works of our maker,
learn of his deeds all-powerful:
wars will cease across the world
when he shatters the spear!
Be still and know your creator,
uplift him in the nations –
God the Lord of hosts is with us evermore!

48 Graham Kendrick
© 1985 Thankyou Music

1 God is the strength of my life,
    my joy, my song;
I will sing praises to him
    and rejoice.
He has done great things for me
    out of his mercy:
O that the nations might see
    that he is Lord!
    Show us your strength, O God,
    summon now your power, O Lord;
    show us your strength, O God,
    may your kingdom come, O Lord!

2 Stir up your strength, O God,
    come near to save;
let Satan's strongholds fall down
    in Jesus' name.
Come set the prisoners free,
    bring joy and gladness;
now let your enemies see,
    that Christ is Lord.
    Show us your strength . . .

49 Graham Kendrick
© 1985 Thankyou Music

God is good – we sing and shout it,
God is good – we celebrate;
God is good – no more we doubt it,
God is good – we know it's true!

And when I think of his love for me,
my heart fills with praise
and I feel like dancing;
for in his heart there is room for me,
and I run with arms open wide.
    God is good . . .

50 P Dearmer (1867–1936)

1 God is love – his the care,
tending each, everywhere;
God is love – all is there!
Jesus came to show him,
that we all might know him:
    Sing aloud, loud, loud;
    sing aloud, loud, loud:
    God is good,
    God is truth, God is beauty –
    praise him!

2 Jesus shared all our pain,
lived and died, rose again,
rules our hearts, now as then –
for he came to save us
by the truth he gave us:
    Sing aloud . . .

3 To our Lord praise we sing –
light and life, friend and king,
coming down love to bring,
pattern for our duty,
showing God in beauty:
    Sing aloud . . .

50A PRAISE SHOUT
From Psalm 117

LEADER Praise the Lord, all you nations;
ALL **extol him all you peoples!**

LEADER For his love protecting us is strong;
ALL **his faithfulness endures for ever!**

51 Dave Fellingham
© 1982 Thankyou Music

God of glory, we exalt your name,
you who reign in majesty;
we lift our hearts to you
and we will worship, praise and magnify
your holy name.

In power resplendent
you reign in glory;
eternal King, you reign for ever:
your word is mighty,
releasing captives,
your love is gracious –
you are my God.

52

From Psalm 85
Jacques Berthier
© Taizé. Used by permission of Wm Collins

ALL: CONTINUOUS RESPONSE
Grant to us your peace, Lord
grant to us . . .

Dona nobis pacem,
dona nobis pacem.

1 SOLO
Lamb of God,
you take away the sins of the world:
have mercy on us.

Lamb of God . . .

Lamb of God,
you take away the sins of the world:
grant us peace!

OTHER VERSES

2 I will hear what the Lord has to say –
a voice that speaks of peace;
peace for his people and peace for his friends,
and peace for those
who turn to him in their hearts.

3 His help is near for those who adore him,
his glory will dwell in our land.

4 Mercy and faithfulness have met,
justice and peace have embraced;
faithfulness shall spring from the earth,
and justice look down from heaven.

5 The Lord will grant us his joy,
and our earth shall yield its fruit;
justice shall walk before him,
and peace shall follow his steps.

53

© 1966 Willard Jabusch

God has spoken to his people
Alleluia,
and his words are words of wisdom.
alleluia!

1 Open your ears, O Christian people,
open your ears and hear good news;
open your hearts, O royal priesthood,
God has come to you, God has come to you.
God has spoken . . .

2 They who have ears to hear his message,
they who have ears, then let them hear;
they who would learn the way of wisdom,
let them hear God's word,
let them hear God's word!
God has spoken . . .

3 Israel comes to greet the saviour,
Judah is glad to see his day;
from east and west the peoples travel,
he will show the way, he will show the way.
God has spoken . . .

54

T O Chisholm (1866–1960)
© 1923, 1951, Hope Publishing Co.
This version © 1982 Jubilate Hymns † / Hope Publishing Co.

1 Great is your faithfulness,
O God my Father,
you have fulfilled
all your promise to me;
you never fail
and your love is unchanging –
all you have been
you for ever will be.
Great is your faithfulness,
great is your faithfulness,
morning by morning
new mercies I see;
all I have needed
your hand has provided –
great is your faithfulness,
Father, to me.

2 Summer and winter,
and springtime and harvest,
sun, moon and stars
in their courses above
join with all nature
in eloquent witness
to your great faithfulness,
mercy and love.
Great is your faithfulness . . .

3 Pardon for sin,
and a peace everlasting,
your living presence
to cheer and to guide;
strength for today,
and bright hope for tomorrow –
these are the blessings
your love will provide.
Great is your faithfulness . . .

55

From Revelation 15
derived from the 'Daily Office'
© Joint Liturgical Group

Great and wonderful are your deeds,
Lord God, the almighty;
just and true are your ways,
O King of the nations!

1 Who shall not revere
and praise your name, O Lord?
For you alone are holy.
Great and wonderful . . .

2 All nations shall come
and worship in your presence,
for your just dealings
have been revealed.
Great and wonderful . . .

To him who sits on the throne
and to the Lamb,
to the Lamb:
be praise and honour,
glory and might,
for ever and ever.
Amen, amen, amen.

56

© Christopher Porteous
and in this version Jubilate Hymns †

1 He gave his life in selfless love,
   for sinners once he came;
he had no stain of sin himself
   but bore our guilt and shame:
he took the cup of pain and death,
   his blood was freely shed;
we see his body on the cross,
   we share the living bread.

2 He did not come to call the good
   but sinners to repent;
it was the lame, the deaf, the blind
   for whom his life was spent:
to heal the sick, to find the lost –
   it was for such he came,
and round his table all may come
   to praise his holy name.

3 They heard him call his Father's name –
   then 'Finished!' was his cry;
like them we have forsaken him
   and left him there to die:
the sins that crucified him then
   are sins his blood has cured;
the love that bound him to a cross
   our freedom has ensured.

4 His body broken once for us
   is glorious now above;
the cup of blessing we receive,
   a sharing of his love:
as in his presence we partake,
   his dying we proclaim
until the hour of majesty
   when Jesus comes again.

57

From Psalm 32.1–6
Bill Batstone
© 1984 Word Music (UK)

Happy is the one whose sin
freely is forgiven,
whose innocence has been declared
by the Lord of heaven.
Happy is the one . . .

1 I cried till I could cry no more
when my guilt in me remained;
I fell beneath the burning sun
till forgiveness brought the rain.
   Happy is the one . . .

2 When I let my heart be known
   my confession made,
   I saw your mercy flow
   h my guilt away.
   y is the one . . .

3 People, let your voice be heard
in prayer before your God:
he alone can rescue you
from trouble like a flood.
   Happy is the one . . .

58

Graham Kendrick
© 1987 Make Way Music / Thankyou Music

He has shown you, O man, what is good –
and what does the Lord require of you?
He has shown you, O man, what is good –
and what does the Lord require of you,
but to act justly, and to love mercy,
and to walk humbly with your God;
but to act justly, and to love mercy,
and to walk humbly with your God.

He has shown . . .

58A

PRAISE SHOUT
From Psalm 103

LEADER Praise the Lord, O my soul;
ALL **all my being, praise his name!**

LEADER Praise the Lord, O my soul;
ALL **and forget not all his blessings!**

LEADER Praise the Lord, O my soul.
ALL **Praise the Lord! Amen.**

59

verse 1: © Marvin Frey
verse 3: © Michael Baughen / Jubilate Hymns †

1 He is Lord, he is Lord,
he is risen from the dead
   and he is Lord!
Every knee shall bow,
every tongue confess
that Jesus Christ is Lord.

2 He's my Lord, he's my Lord,
he is risen from the dead
   and he's my Lord!
Every knee shall bow,
every tongue confess
that Jesus Christ is Lord.

3 He will come, he will come,
he has promised in his word
   that he will come;
some glad day or night,
with great power and might,
the risen Lord will come.

60

Unknown
© Copyright controlled

He is risen, risen, risen;
he is risen, risen – the Lord:
he is risen, risen, risen;
he is risen, risen – the Lord!

1 LEADER Oh be joyful –
ALL join in praise and sing:
O alleluia!

LEADER	We were all dead;
ALL	we now live in Jesus:
	O alleluia!
	He is risen . . .

2 LEADER Over death's power
ALL Jesus has overcome:
O alleluia!
LEADER Life eternal
ALL Jesus has given us:
O alleluia!
He is risen . . .

3 LEADER Alleluia!
ALL All Christians, join us now:
O alleluia!
LEADER He's triumphant!
ALL All Christians, praise him now,
O alleluia!

Alleluia, -luia, -luia;
alleluia – life is come:
he is risen, risen, risen;
he is risen, risen – the Lord!

61
Graham Kendrick
© 1986 Thankyou Music

He that is in us is greater
than he that is in the world;
he that is in us is greater
than he that is in the world.

1 Therefore I will sing and I will rejoice
for his Spirit lives in me:
Christ the living One has overcome,
and we share in his victory.
He that is in us . . .

2 All the powers of death and hell and sin
lie crushed beneath his feet:
Jesus owns the name above all names,
crowned with honour and majesty.
He that is in us . . .

62
Unknown
© Marshall, Morgan & Scott

1 He's got the whole world
in his hands,
he's got the whole wide world
in his hands,
he's got the whole world
in his hands,
he's got the whole world
in his hands!

2 He's got everybody here
in his hands . . .

3 WOMEN
He's got you and me, sister,
in his hands . . .

4 MEN
He's got you and me, brother,
in his hands . . .

5 ALL
He's got the whole world
in his hands . . .

63
Chris Bowater
© 1981 Word Music (UK)

Here I am, wholly available –
as for me, I will serve the Lord.

1 The fields are white unto harvest
but oh, the labourers are so few;
so Lord I give myself to help the reaping,
to gather precious souls unto you.
Here I am . . .

2 The time is right in the nation
for works of power and authority;
God's looking for a people who are willing
to be counted in his glorious victory.
Here I am . . .

3 As salt are we ready to savour,
in darkness are we ready to be light;
God's seeking out a very special people
to manifest his truth and his might.
Here I am . . .

64
From Revelation 4

1 Holy, holy, holy is the Lord;
holy is the Lord God almighty!
Holy, holy, holy is the Lord;
holy is the Lord God almighty
who was, and is, and is to come!
Holy, holy, holy is the Lord!

2 Jesus, Jesus, Jesus is the Lord;
Jesus is the Lord God almighty . . .

3 Worthy, worthy, worthy is the Lord;
worthy is the Lord God almighty . . .

4 Glory, glory, glory to the Lord;
glory to the Lord God almighty . . .

65
From Psalm 123
Jacques Berthier
© Taizé. Used by permission of Wm Collins

CONTINUOUS RESPONSE
Holy Lord, have mercy on us all,
Lord have mercy on us;
Holy Lord . . .

OR

*Miserere nobis Domine,
miserere nobis;
miserere nobis Domine,
miserere nobis.*

1 SOLO
Behold, as the eyes of servants
are on the hands of their masters:

2 SOLO
Our eyes are fixed on the Lord our God
until he shows us his mercy.

66

Jacques Berthier
© Taizé. Used by permission of Wm Collins

CONTINUOUS RESPONSE

Holy, holy, holy Lord,
holy, holy, holy Lord!

OR:

Hosanna in the highest,
hosanna in the highest!

OR:

Sanctus, sanctus, Dominus,
sanctus, sanctus, Dominus!

OR:

Hosanna in excelsis,
hosanna in excelsis!

1 SOLO

Holy, holy, holy Lord,
God of power and might,
heaven and earth
are full of your glory.
Hosanna in the highest!

2 SOLO

I will bless the Lord at all times,
his praise
shall always be on my lips:
glorify the Lord with me,
together let us praise his name!

67

Jacques Berthier
© Taizé. Used by permission of Wm Collins

CONTINUOUS RESPONSE

Holy Spirit, come to us;
Holy Spirit, come to us!

OR:

Veni, Sancte Spiritus;
Veni, Sancte Spiritus.

1 SOLO

Come, Holy Spirit, from heaven
shine forth with your glorious light –
Holy Spirit, come to us.
Holy Spirit . . .

2 SOLO

Come, Father of the poor;
come, generous Spirit,
come, light of our hearts –
Holy Spirit, come to us.
Holy Spirit . . .

68

Chris Bowater
© 1986 Word Music (UK)

1 Holy Spirit, we welcome you,
Holy Spirit, we welcome you!
Move among us with holy fire
as we lay aside all earthly desire,
hands reach out and our hearts aspire.
Holy Spirit, Holy Spirit,
Holy Spirit, we welcome you!

2 Holy Spirit, we welcome you,
Holy Spirit, we welcome you!
Let the breeze of your presence blow
that your children here might truly know
how to move in the Spirit's flow.
Holy Spirit, Holy Spirit,
Holy Spirit, we welcome you!

3 Holy Spirit, we welcome you,
Holy Spirit, we welcome you!
Please accomplish in us today
some new work of loving grace, we pray –
unreservedly – have your way.
Holy Spirit, Holy Spirit,
Holy Spirit, we welcome you!

69

Keith Green
© 1982 Birdwing Music / Cherry Lane Music

How I love you:
you are the One,
you are the One;
how I love you:
you are the One for me!

1 I was so lost,
but you showed the way –
for you are the Way;
I was so lost,
but you showed the way to me.
How I love you . . .

2 I was lied to,
but you told the truth –
for you are the Truth;
I was lied to,
but you showed the truth to me.
How I love you . . .

3 I was dying,
but you gave me life –
for you are the Life;
I was dying,
but you gave your life for me.
How I love you:
you are the One,
you are the One;
how I love you:
you are the One –
God's risen Son,
you are the One for me!

4 Alleluia,
you are the One,
you are the One;
alleluia,
you are the One for me!
How I love you . . .

70
From Psalm 84
Tom Howard
© 1982 Maranatha! Music / Word Music (UK)

1 How lovely is your dwelling-place,
almighty Lord!
There's a hunger deep inside my soul:
only in your presence
are my heart and flesh restored –
how lovely.
> How lovely is your dwelling-place,
> almighty Lord!
> There's a hunger deep inside my soul:
> only in your presence
> are my heart and flesh restored,
> how lovely is your dwelling place.

2 In your courts there's shelter
for the greatest and the small;
the sparrow has a place to build her nest,
the pilgrim finds refreshment
in the rains that fall;
and each one has the strength
to meet the test.
> How lovely . . .

3 A single day is better
when spent in humble praise,
than a thousand days of living
without you:
the Lord bestows his favour
on each one who obeys
and blessings on the one
whose heart is true.
> How lovely . . .

71
From Isaiah 52
Leonard E Smith Jnr
© 1974, 1978 Thankyou Music

1 How lovely on the mountains are the feet of him
who brings good news, good news,
proclaiming peace,
announcing news of happiness:
our God reigns, our God reigns!
> Our God reigns, our God reigns,
> our God reigns, our God reigns!

2 You watchmen lift your voices joyfully as one,
shout for your king, your king;
see eye to eye the Lord restoring Zion:
your God reigns, your God reigns!
> Your God . . .

3 Waste places of Jerusalem
break forth with joy –
we are redeemed, redeemed;
the Lord has saved and comforted his people:
your God reigns, your God reigns!
> Your God . . .

4 Ends of the earth,
see the salvation of your God –
Jesus is Lord, is Lord!
Before the nations he has bared his holy arm:
your God reigns, your God reigns!
> Your God . . .

72
Carl Tuttle
© 1985 Mercy Publishing / Thankyou Music

1 Hosanna, hosanna, hosanna in the highest.
Hosanna, hosanna, hosanna in the highest.
Lord, we lift up your name,
with hearts full of praise.
Be exalted, O Lord my God –
hosanna in the highest.

2 Glory, glory, glory to the King of kings;
glory, glory, glory to the King of kings:
Lord, we lift up your name
with hearts full of praise.
Be exalted, O Lord my God –
glory to the King of kings.

73
Chris Eaton
© 1983 Patch Music

1 I see perfection as I look in your eyes, Lord;
there's no rejection as I look in your eyes, Lord.
> You are a river that is never dry,
> you are the star that lights the evening sky,
> you are my God and I will follow you,
> and now I know just where I'm going to.

> We are children, children of the King
> we will praise your name,
> glorify you, magnify you
> Jesus, we can never deny
> your love for us on the cross
> now you've made us children of the King.

Your Holy Spirit will for ever control me!
I give my present, future, past,
to you completely.
> You are a river . . .
> We are children . . .

> Now you've made us children of the King!

74
Dave Bilbrough
© 1983 Thankyou Music

I am a new creation,
no more in condemnation,
here in the grace of God I stand;
my heart is overflowing,
my love just keeps on growing,
here in the grace of God I stand:
and I will praise you, Lord,
yes I will praise you, Lord,
and I will sing of all that you have done.

A joy that knows no limit,
a lightness in my spirit –
here in the grace of God I stand.

75
From Psalm 130
Bill Batstone
© 1986 Maranatha! Music / Word Music (UK)

1 I call to you from out of the deep,
O Lord, most high;
aware of my sin and the distance I keep
from the Light, O Lord.

But there is forgiveness with you!
In wonder I fall on my knees;
my soul waits for the Lord
in the hope of his promise –
in the hope of his promise
deliverance will come.
My soul waits for the Lord
through the night to the morning,
like a night-watchman waiting
for the coming of the dawn.

2 Look to the Lord all you people in need,
for he is kind;
he will break the chains of your soul's slavery –
for all time, O Lord.
But there is forgiveness . . .

3 Tell me who could stand
in the Lord's righteous reckoning
if our lives faced his light?
Then, if all our deeds were revealed
at God's beckoning,
who could hold their head high?
But there is forgiveness . . .

76
Michael Card
© 1981 Whole Armor Publishing / Cherry Pie Music

I have decided
I'm going to live like a believer,
turn my back on the deceiver,
going to live what I believe:
I have decided
being good is just a fable –
I just can't 'cause I'm not able,
going to leave it to the Lord.

1 There's a wealth of things that I professed,
I said that I believed,
but deep inside I never changed,
I guess I'd been deceived,
a voice inside kept telling me
that I'd change by and by,
but the Spirit made it clear to me
that kind of life's a lie.
I have decided . . .

2 So, forget the game of being good
and all self-righteous things,
'cause the only good inside your heart
is the good that Jesus brings;
when the world begins to see you change,
don't expect them to applaud,
keep your eyes on him and tell yourself
I've begun the work of God.
I have decided . . .

77
Gary Houston
© 1987 Thankyou Music

ove, I love you, Jesus,
ve, I love you, Jesus;
are the light within me:
you, I love you, Jesus!

ou, I love you, Jesus . . .

I will sing a new song to you, Lord,
I will lift my hands to you;
I'll sing and tell the world
that you're my king
and you're the one who saved me:
you're my strength and my rock –
O Lord, you're beautiful!

I love you, I love you, Jesus . . .

78
From Psalm 18
© Christopher Idle / Jubilate Hymns †

1 I love you, O Lord, you alone,
my refuge on whom I depend;
my maker, my saviour, my own,
my hope and my trust without end:
the Lord is my strength and my song,
defender and guide of my ways;
my master to whom I belong,
my God who shall have all my praise.

2 The dangers of death gathered round,
the waves of destruction came near;
but in my despairing I found
the Lord who released me from fear:
I called for his help in my pain,
to God my salvation I cried;
he brought me his comfort again,
I live by the strength he supplied.

3 My hope is the promise he gives,
my life is secure in his hand;
I shall not be lost, for he lives!
he comes to my aid – I shall stand!
Lord God, you are powerful to save,
your Spirit will spur me to pray;
your Son has defeated the grave:
I trust and I praise you today!

79
From Psalm 62
John Daniels
© 1985 Ears and Eyes Music

I rest in God alone,
from him comes my salvation;
my soul finds rest in him,
my fortress – I'll not be shaken.

1 My hope is in the Lord
my honour and strength;
my refuge is in him for ever,
my trust and all of my heart –
in him alone my soul finds rest.
I rest in God alone . . .

2 O trust in him, you people,
pour out your hearts,
for God is our refuge for ever,
my trust and all of my heart –
in him alone my soul finds rest.
O trust in him, you people . . .

80

after Christoph Haus, Burkhard Bahr
and Joachim Gnep
© Michael Perry / Jubilate Hymns †

I tell you . . .
Jesus is all that you need,
Jesus – hear what I say!
Jesus – I tell you, he is the Life:
he is the Truth and the Way.
I tell you . . .

1 Once I was dissatisfied
and tired of standing still;
tasting pleasure far and wide,
I'd just had my fill.
Then I met the One who died –
now risen from the dead –
Jesus Christ, the Crucified:
he gave me life instead!
   I tell you . . .

2 Once I walked the road alone,
and tried hard to be brave –
for, you see, I'd never known
that Jesus can save.
Now with him upon the throne
I all my days will spend
gladly telling everyone
that Jesus is their Friend!
   I tell you . . .

81

From Psalm 121
Bill Batstone
© 1984 Maranatha! Music / Word Music (UK)

1 I look up to the mountains,
   to the hills I turn my eyes:
who will come to help me,
   can I find a place to hide?
The One who made the heavens
   and the earth will hear my call,
the Lord will come to help me
   and he will not let me fall.
   He will not let you fall,
   he will not let you fall;
   he is never weary,
   and he will not let you fall.

   He will not . . .

2 The One who watches Israel
   will his vigil keep,
through the burning sunlight
   and in the darkness deep;
constantly beside you –
   you need not fear at all,
the Lord is there to help you,
   and he will not let you fall.
   He will not . . .

3 So when you are in danger,
   when by trouble you are found,
and your very soul is threatened
   by the evil all around;
in all of your ways
   and in your troubles great and small,
now and ever after
   he will not let you fall.
   He will not . . .

82

Chris Rolinson
© 1988 Thankyou Music

1 I want to serve you, Lord, in total abandonment,
I want to yield my heart to you;
I want to give my life in all surrender,
I want to live for you alone.

2 I want to give my all in total abandonment,
releasing all within my grasp;
I want to live my life in all its fulness,
I want to worship Christ alone.

3 I want to come to you in total abandonment –
Lord, will you set my heart ablaze?
I want to love you with all my soul and strength,
I want to give you all my days.

83

Tim Mayfield
© 1987 Thankyou Music

I want to sing a praise song to you,
I want to lift the name of Jesus higher;
I want to sing, I want to move my feet –
Lord, I'm going to worship you!

   I want to praise, praise you Lord,
   I want to praise, praise you Lord,
   I want to praise you Lord:
   you're worthy to be praised –
   praise the Lord with me!

84

Graham Kendrick
© 1988 Make Way Music / Thankyou Music

MEN   'I will build my church,
WOMEN   I will build my church,
MEN   and the gates of hell,
WOMEN   and the gates of hell,
MEN   shall not prevail,
WOMEN   shall not prevail,
ALL   against it.'
MEN   I will build . . .

ALL
So you powers in the heavens above,
bow down!
And you powers on the earth below,
bow down!
And acknowledge that Jesus,
Jesus, Jesus is Lord,
is Lord!

85
Martin Nystrom
© 1984 Hosanna! Music / Frontier Music

I will come and bow down at your feet,
    Lord Jesus;
in you presence is fulness of joy.
There is nothing,
        there is no-one to compare with you:
I take pleasure in worshipping you, Lord.

86
Rob Hayward
© 1985 Thankyou Music

I'm accepted, I'm forgiven,
I am fathered by the true and living God:
I'm accepted – no condemnation,
I am loved by the true and living God.
    There's no guilt or fear
    as I draw near
to the saviour and creator of the world;
    there is joy and peace
    as I release
my worship to you, O Lord.

87
Graham Kendrick
© 1987 Make Way Music / Thankyou Music

If my people who bear my name,
will humble themselves and pray;
if they seek my presence
and turn their backs on their wicked ways;
then I will hear from heaven,
I'll hear from heaven and will forgive.
I will forgive their sins
and will heal their land –
yes I will heal their land.

88
W C Smith (1824–1908)
© in this version Jubilate Hymns †

1 Immortal, invisible, God
        only wise,
    in light inaccessible
        hid from our eyes;
    most holy, most glorious,
        the ancient of days,
    almighty, victorious,
        your great name we praise.

2 Unresting, unhasting,
        and silent as light,
    nor wanting nor wasting,
        you rule us in might;
    your justice like mountains
        high soaring above,
    your clouds which are fountains
        of goodness and love.

3 To all life you give, Lord,
        to both great and small,
    in all life you live, Lord,
        the true life of all:
    we blossom and flourish,
        uncertain and frail;
    we wither and perish,
        but you never fail.

4 We worship before you,
        great Father of light,
    while angels adore you,
        all veiling their sight;
    our praises we render,
        O Father, to you
    whom only the splendour of light
        hides from view.

88A
PRAISE SHOUT
From Psalm 8

LEADER O Lord, our Lord,
ALL **how glorious is your name
in all the earth!**

LEADER High above the heavens
ALL **your majesty is praised.
Alleluia!**

89
Bob Kilpatrick
© Prism Tree Music

1 In my life, Lord,
        be glorified, be glorified;
    in my life, Lord,
        be glorified today!

2 In my song, Lord,
        be glorified, be glorified;
    in my song, Lord,
        be glorified today!

3 In your church, Lord,
        be glorified, be glorified;
    in your church, Lord,
        be glorified today!

4 In my speech, Lord,
        be glorified, be glorified;
    in my speech, Lord,
        be glorified today!

90
Jamie Owens-Collins
© 1984 Fairhill Music / Word Music (UK)

1 In heavenly armour we'll enter the land –
    the battle belongs to the Lord;
    no weapon that's fashioned against us
        will stand –
    the battle belongs to the Lord.
        And we sing glory, honour,
        power and strength to the Lord;
        we sing glory, honour,
        power and strength to the Lord!

2 When the power of darkness
        comes in like a flood,
    the battle belongs to the Lord;
    he's raised up a standard,
        the power of his blood –
    the battle belongs to the Lord.
        And we sing glory . . .

3 When your enemy presses in hard,
        do not fear –
the battle belongs to the Lord;
take courage, my friend,
        your redemption is near –
the battle belongs to the Lord.
    And we sing glory . . .
    And we sing glory . . .
    Power and strength to the Lord,
    power and strength to the Lord!

91
Garth Hewitt
© 1985 Word Music (UK) †

1 It was raining down in Memphis
on the night before he died –
a shot of hate would come tomorrow,
may'be that's why he cried:
    Light a candle in the darkness,
    light a candle in the night;
    let the love of Jesus light us,
    light a candle in the night.

2 On a Wednesday in Kampala,
there they shot Janani down;
he stood firm against the evil,
he paid the price, he won the crown.
    Like a candle . . .

3 It was on the Monday evening
in the town San Salvador,
that he took the fatal bullet
all because he loved the poor.
    Like a candle . . .

4 The world grew dark upon a Friday,
creation held its breath in fear:
by the wounds that he was given
we are healed if we draw near.
    Like a candle . . .

5 Angels sang upon a Sunday,
the Devil moaned and turned aside:
a blaze of glory from an empty tomb.
Death itself has had to die!
    Like a candle . . .

92
Brent Chambers
© 1977 Scripture in Song / Thankyou Music

In the presence of your people
    I will praise your name,
for alone you are holy,
    enthroned on the praises of Israel.
Let us celebrate your goodness
    and your steadfast love;
may your name be exalted
    here on earth and in heaven above!

93
Wendy Churchill
© 1981 Springtide / Words Music (UK)

1 Jesus is king,
    and we will extol him,
give him the glory,
    and honour his name;
he reigns on high,
    enthroned in the heavens –
Word of the Father,
    exalted for us.

2 We have a hope
    that is steadfast and certain,
gone through the curtain
    and touching the throne;
we have a Priest
    who is there interceding,
pouring his grace
    on our lives day by day.

3 We come to him
    our Priest and Apostle,
clothed in his glory
    and bearing his name,
laying our lives
    with gladness before him –
filled with his Spirit
    we worship the King:

4 'O Holy One,
    our hearts do adore you;
thrilled with your goodness
    we give you our praise!'
Angels in light
    with worship surround him,
Jesus, our Saviour,
    for ever the same.

94
Ian Smale
© 1987 Thankyou Music

1 Jehovah Jireh – God will provide,
Jehovah Rophe – God heals;
Jehovah M'keddesh – God who sanctifies,
Jehovah Nissi – God is my banner.

2 Jehovah Rohi – God, my shepherd,
Jehovah Shalom – God is peace;
Jehovah Tsidkenu – God, our righteousness,
Jehovah Shammah – God who is there.

95
Jonathan Wallis
© 1983 Thankyou Music

1 Jesus has sat down at God's right hand,
he is reigning now on David's throne;
God has placed all things beneath his feet,
his enemies will be his footstool.
    For the government
    is now upon his shoulder,
    for the government
    is now upon his shoulder;
    and of the increase
    of his government and peace
    there will be no end,
    there will be no end,
    there will be no end.

2 God has now exalted him on high,
given him a name above all names;
every knee will bow, and tongue confess
that Jesus Christ is Lord.
  For the government
  is now upon his shoulder,
  for the government
  is now upon his shoulder;
  and of the increase
  of his government and peace
  there will be no end,
  there will be no end,
  there will be no end.

3 Jesus is now living in his church:
those who have been purchased by his blood –
they will serve their God, a royal priesthood,
and they will reign on earth.
  For the government . . .

4 Sound the trumpets – good news to the poor!
Captives will go free, the blind will see;
the kingdom of this world will soon become
the kingdom of our God.
  For the government . . .

96 Tom Colvin

Jesus, Jesus, fill us with your love;
show us how to serve
the neighbours we have from you.

1 Kneels at the feet of his friends,
silently washes their feet –
Master who acts as a slave to them:
  Jesus, Jesus . . .

2 Neighbours are rich folk and poor;
neighbours are black, brown and white;
neighbours are nearby and far away:
  Jesus, Jesus . . .

3 These are the ones we should serve,
these are the ones we should love;
all these are neighbours to us and you:
  Jesus, Jesus . . .

4 Loving puts us on our knees,
serving as though we were slaves –
this is the way we should live with you:
  Jesus, Jesus . . .

97 I Watts (1674–1748)
© in this version Jubilate Hymns †

1 Jesus shall reign where'er the sun
does his successive journeys run;
his kingdom stretch from shore to shore
till moons shall rise and set no more.

2 People and realms of every tongue
declare his love in sweetest song,
and children's voices shall proclaim
their early blessings on his name.

3 Blessings abound where Jesus reigns –
the prisoner leaps to lose his chains,
the weary find eternal rest,
the hungry and the poor are blessed.

4 To him shall endless prayer be made,
and princes throng to crown his head;
his name like incense shall arise
with every morning sacrifice.

5 Let all creation rise and bring
the highest honours to our king;
angels descend with songs again
and earth repeat the loud 'Amen!'

98 Paul Kyle
© 1980 Thankyou Music

Jesus, we enthrone you,
we proclaim you our king –
standing here in the midst of us!
We raise you up with our praise.
  And as we worship, build a throne,
  and as we worship, build a throne,
  and as we worship, build a throne –
  come, Lord Jesus, and take your place!

99 Dave Fellingham
© 1985 Thankyou Music

Jesus,
you are the radiance
of the Father's glory,
you are the Son,
the appointed heir,
through whom all things are made;
you are the one
who sustains all things
by your powerful word,
you have purified us from sin,
you are exalted, O Lord,
exalted, O Lord
to the right hand of God:

Jesus, you are . . .

  Crowned with glory,
  crowned with honour –
  we worship you!

100 Dave Fellingham
© 1987 Thankyou Music

Jesus, you have lifted me,
given me your life;
you have heard my cry to you,
you have raised me up.
My heart trusts in you and I am helped;
you're my strength and shield.
My heart will rejoice,
and with my song I thank you, Lord.
You're my fortress and my rock –
I shall not be moved;
my life's hidden now with Christ in God –
I am now secure.

101

C Elliott (1789–1871)
© in this version Jubilate Hymns †

1 Just as I am, without one plea
but that you died to set me free,
and at your bidding 'Come to me!'
O Lamb of God, I come, I come.

2 Just as I am, without delay
your call of mercy I obey –
your blood can wash my sins away:
O Lamb of God, I come, I come.

3 Just as I am, though tossed about
with many a conflict, many a doubt,
fightings within and fears without,
O Lamb of God, I come, I come.

4 Just as I am, poor, wretched, blind!
Sight, riches, healing of the mind –
all that I need, in you to find:
O Lamb of God, I come, I come.

5 Just as I am! You will receive,
will welcome, pardon, cleanse, relieve:
because your promise I believe,
O Lamb of God, I come, I come.

6 Just as I am! Your love unknown
has broken every barrier down:
now to be yours, yes, yours alone,
O Lamb of God, I come, I come.

7 Just as I am! Of that free love
the breadth, length, depth and height to prove,
here for a time and then above,
O Lamb of God, I come, I come.

101A

PRAISE SHOUT
From Psalm 106

LEADER Give thanks to the Lord, for he is good;
ALL **his love endures for ever.**

LEADER Tell of all his mighty acts;
ALL **and make his praises heard.**

LEADER Praise be to the Lord, the God of Israel:
ALL **from everlasting to everlasting.**

LEADER Let all the people say, 'Amen':
ALL **Amen, praise the Lord!**

102

I Watts (1674–1748)

1 Joy to the world! The Lord has come:
let earth receive her king,
let every heart prepare him room
and heaven and nature sing,
and heaven and nature sing,
and heaven, and heaven and nature sing!

2 Joy to the earth! The saviour reigns:
your sweetest songs employ
while fields and streams and hills and plains
repeat the sounding joy,
repeat the sounding joy,
repeat, repeat the sounding joy.

3 He rules the world with truth and grace,
and makes the nations prove
the glories of his righteousness,
the wonders of his love,
the wonders of his love,
the wonders, wonders of his love.

103

Sophie Conty and Naomi Batya
© 1980 Maranatha! Music (USA) / Word Music (UK)

King of kings and Lord of lords,
Glory, alleluia!
King of kings . . .
Jesus, Prince of peace,
Glory, alleluia!
Jesus, Prince . . .

104

Graham Kendrick
© 1988 Make Way Music / Thankyou Music

King of kings, Lord of lords,
Lion of Judah, Word of God.

King of kings . . .

And here he comes, the King of glory comes,
in righteousness he comes to judge the earth;
and here he comes, the King of glory comes –
with justice he'll rule the earth!

105

Graham Kendrick
© 1983 Thankyou Music

1 Led like a lamb to the slaughter
in silence and shame,
there on your back
you carried a world
of violence and pain,
bleeding, dying,
bleeding, dying.
You're alive – you're alive,
you have risen –
Alleluia . . .
and the power
and the glory is given –
alleluia . . .
Jesus to you.

2 At break of dawn – poor Mary,
still weeping, she came:
when through her grief
she heard your voice
now speaking her name,
MEN 'Mary!' WOMEN 'Master!'
MEN 'Mary!' WOMEN 'Master!'
You're alive . . .

3 At the right hand of the Father,
now seated on high,
you have begun your eternal reign
of justice and joy:
Glory, glory,
glory, glory!
You're alive . . .

106

Brent Chambers
© 1979 Scripture in Song / Thankyou Music

Let our praise to you be as incense,
let our praise to you be as pillars of your throne;
let our praise to you be as incense,
as we come before you
  and worship you alone –
as we see you in your splendour,
as we gaze upon your majesty,
as we join the hosts of angels
and proclaim together your holiness:
  Holy, holy, holy;
  holy is the Lord!
  Holy, holy, holy;
  holy is the Lord!

107

© 1987 Phil Pringle / Thankyou Music

Let the heavens shout for joy,
let the earth bring forth its praise,
let the seas roar, for my Saviour comes;
let the nations bow their knees,
fall in awe upon their face,
see him come in clouds of righteousness.
  Alleluia, alleluia, alleluia –
  let the world sing: Jesus reigns;
  alleluia, alleluia, alleluia –
  let the world sing: Jesus reigns!

108

Dave Bilbrough
© 1979 Thankyou Music

Let there be love shared among us,
let there be love in our eyes;
may now your love sweep this nation,
cause us, O Lord, to arise:
give us a fresh understanding
of brotherly love that is real;
let there be love shared among us,
let there be love!

109

Steven Fry
© Birdwing Music / Cherry Lane Music

Lift up your heads to the coming King;
bow before him and adore him,
  sing to his majesty:
let your praises be pure and holy,
giving glory to the King of kings.

110

Stephen Chapman
© 1984 Paragon Music / Cherry Pie Music

1 Lift your voice and sing –
  we serve the living King;
  our lives are the throne
  where his glory shown
  will draw people to Jesus.
    Give him the glory
    and honour and praise:
    he is the Lord
    of creation always –
    almighty God,
    worthy alone to be praised!

2 Lift your eyes and see
  his power and majesty!
  Our lives are the throne
  where his glory shown
  will draw people to Jesus.
    Give him the glory
    and honour and praise:
    he is the King
    of creation always –
    almighty God,
    worthy alone to be praised!

3 Every eye will behold him,
  every knee bow in prayer,
  every tongue will confess him,
  and all the earth will proclaim he is Lord.
    Give him the glory
    and honour and praise:
    he is the King
    of creation always –
    almighty God,
    worthy alone to be praised!

    Give him the glory
    and honour and praise:
    he is the Lord
    of creation always –
    almighty God,
    worthy alone to be praised,
    worthy alone to be praised,
    worthy alone to be praised!

111

Graham Kendrick
© 1988 Make Way Music / Thankyou Music

1 Light has dawned that ever shall blaze,
  darkness flees away;
  Christ the light has shone in our hearts,
  turning night to day.
    We proclaim him King of kings,
    we lift high his name;
    heaven and earth shall bow at his feet,
    when he comes to reign.

2 WOMEN
  Saviour of the world is he,
  heaven's king come down;
  judgement, love and mercy meet
  at his thorny crown.
    ALL We proclaim . . .

3 MEN
  Life has sprung from hearts of stone,
  by the Spirit's breath;
  hell shall let her captives go,
  life has conquered death.
    ALL We proclaim . . .

4 Blood has flowed that cleanses from sin,
  God his love has proved;
  man may mock and demons may rage –
  we shall not be moved!
    We proclaim . . .

    We proclaim . . .

112

From The Alternative Service Book
© 1980 The Central Board of Finance
of the Church of England

SOLO Lighten our darkness, Lord, we pray,
ALL lighten our darkness, Lord, we pray;
SOLO and in your mercy defend us,
ALL and in your mercy defend us
SOLO from all perils and dangers of this night,
ALL from all perils and dangers of this night;
    for the love of your only Son,
    our Saviour Jesus Christ.
SOLO Amen,
ALL amen,
SOLO amen,
ALL amen!

113

Jodi Page Clark
© 1976 Celebration / Thankyou Music

1 Look around you – can you see:
times are troubled, people grieve?
See the violence, feel the hardness –
all my people, weep with me.
    Kyrie eleison,
    Christe eleison,
    Kyrie eleison.

    OR:

    Father, God, have mercy,
    Jesus, have mercy,
    Spirit, Lord, have mercy!

2 Walk among them – I'll go with you,
reach out to them with my hands:
suffer with me, and together
we will serve them, help them stand.
    Kyrie eleison . . .

3 Forgive us, Father, hear our prayer:
we will walk with you anywhere –
through your suffering, with forgiveness,
take your life into the world.
    Kyrie eleison . . .

113A

PRAISE SHOUT

From Psalm 67

LEADER Let the people praise you, O God;
ALL **let all the people praise you!**

LEADER Let your ways be known on earth;
ALL **your saving power in all the world!**

114

From the Irish
Mary Byrne (1880–1931) and Eleanor Hull (1860–1935)
© in this version Jubilate Hymns †

1 Lord, be my vision, supreme in my heart,
bid every rival give way and depart:
you my best thought in the day or the night,
waking or sleeping your presence my light.

2 Lord, be my wisdom and be my true word,
I ever with you and you with me, Lord:
you my great father and I your true child,
once far away, but by love reconciled.

3 Lord, be my breastplate, my sword for the fight:
be my strong armour, for you are my might;
you are my shelter and you my high tower –
raise me to heaven, O Power of my power.

4 I need no riches, nor earth's empty praise:
you my inheritance through all my days;
all of your treasure to me you impart,
high King of heaven, the first in my heart.

5 High King of heaven, when battle is done,
grant heaven's joy to me, bright heaven's sun;
Christ of my own heart, whatever befall,
still be my vision, O Ruler of all.

115

Chris Rolinson
© 1987 Thankyou Music

1 Lord, come and heal your church,
take our lives and cleanse with your fire;
let your deliverance flow
as we lift your name up higher.
    We will draw near
    and surrender our fear:
    lift our hands to proclaim,
    'Holy Father, you are here!'

2 Spirit of God, come in
and release our hearts to praise you;
make us whole, for
holy we'll become and serve you,
    We will draw near . . .

3 Show us your power, we pray,
that we may share in your glory:
we shall arise, and go
to proclaim your works most holy.
    We will draw near . . .

116

© Timothy Dudley-Smith

1 Lord, for the years
    your love has kept and guided,
urged and inspired us,
    cheered us on our way,
sought us and saved us,
    pardoned and provided,
Lord of the years,
    we bring our thanks today.

2 Lord, for that word,
    the word of life which fires us,
speaks to our hearts
    and sets our souls ablaze;
teaches and trains,
    rebukes us and inspires us;
Lord of the word,
    receive your people's praise.

3 Lord, for our land,
    in this our generation,
spirits oppressed
    by pleasure, wealth and care;
for young and old,
    for commonwealth and nation,
Lord of our land,
    be pleased to hear our prayer.

4 Lord, for our world;
    when we disown and doubt him,
loveless in strength,
    and comfortless in pain;
hungry and helpless,
    lost indeed without him;
Lord of the world,
    we pray that Christ may reign.

5 Lord, for ourselves;
    in living power remake us –
self on the cross
    and Christ upon the throne,
past put behind us,
    for the future take us,
Lord of our lives,
    to live for Christ alone.

117 © Hugh Sherlock and Michael Saward / Jubilate Hymns †

1 Lord, your church on earth is seeking
power and wisdom from above:
teach us all the art of speaking
with the accents of your love.
We will heed your great commission
sending us to every place –
'Go, baptize, fulfil my mission;
serve with love and share my grace!'

2 You release us from our bondage,
lift the burdens caused by sin;
give new hope, new strength and courage,
grant release from fears within.
Light for darkness, joy for sorrow,
love for hatred, peace for strife –
these and countless blessings follow
as the Spirit gives new life.

3 In the streets of every city
where the bruised and lonely live,
we will show the Saviour's pity
and his longing to forgive.
In all lands and with all races
we will serve, and seek to bring
all the world to render praises
Christ, to you, redeemer King.

118 Graham Kendrick © 1986 Thankyou Music

Lord, have mercy on us,
come and heal our land/*world*.
Cleanse with your fire,
heal with your touch:
    humbly we bow
    and call upon you now.
O Lord, have mercy on us,
O Lord, have mercy on us.

119 Patrick Appleford © 1960 Josef Weinberger Ltd.

1 Lord Jesus Christ, you have come to us,
you are one with us, Mary's son;
cleansing our souls from all their sin,
pouring your love and goodness in:
Jesus, our love for you we sing –
    living Lord!

AT COMMUNION THIS MAY BE SUNG:
2 Lord Jesus Christ, now and every day
teach us how to pray, Son of God;
you have commanded us to do
this in remembrance, Lord, of you:
into our lives your power breaks through –
    living Lord!

3 Lord Jesus Christ, you have come to us,
born as one of us, Mary's son;
led out to die on Calvary,
risen from death to set us free:
living Lord Jesus, help us see
    you are Lord!

4 Lord Jesus Christ, I would come to you,
live my life for you, Son of God;
all your commands I know are true,
your many gifts will make me new:
into my life your power breaks through –
    living Lord!

120 Graham Kendrick © 1987 Make Way Music / Thankyou Music

1 Lord, the light of your love is shining,
in the midst of the darkness, shining:
Jesus, light of the world, shine upon us;
set us free by the truth you now bring us –
shine on me, shine on me.
    Shine, Jesus, shine,
    fill this land with the Father's glory;
    blaze, Spirit, blaze,
    set our hearts on fire.
    Flow, river, flow,
    flood the nations with grace and mercy;
    send forth your word, Lord,
    and let there be light!

2 Lord, I come to your awesome presence,
from the shadows into your radiance;
by your Blood I may enter your brightness:
search me, try me, consume all my darkness
shine on me, shine on me.
    Shine, Jesus, shine . . .

3 As we gaze on your kingly brightness
so our faces display your likeness,
ever changing from glory to glory:
mirrored here, may our lives tell your story –
shine on me, shine on me.
    Shine, Jesus, shine . . .

121

H W Baker (1821–1877)
© in this version Jubilate Hymns †

1 Lord your word shall guide us
and with truth provide us:
teach us to receive it
and with joy believe it.
When our foes are near us,
then your word shall cheer us –
word of consolation,
message of salvation.

2 When the storms distress us
and dark clouds oppress us,
then your word protects us
and its light directs us.
Who can tell the pleasure,
who recount the treasure
by your word imparted
to the simple-hearted?

3 Word of mercy, giving
courage to the living;
word of life, supplying
comfort to the dying:
O that we discerning
its most holy learning,
Lord, may love and fear you –
evermore be near you!

122

R Lowry (1826–1899)

1 Low in the grave he lay,
Jesus my saviour,
waiting the coming day,
Jesus my Lord!
Up from the grave he arose
as the victor over all his foes;
he arose in triumph
from the dark domain,
and he lives for ever
with his saints to reign –
he arose, he arose,
Alleluia – Christ arose!

2 Vainly they guard his bed,
Jesus my saviour,
vainly they seal the dead,
Jesus my Lord!
Up from the grave he arose . . .

3 Death cannot keep his prey,
Jesus, my saviour,
he tore the bars away,
Jesus my Lord!
Up from the grave he arose . . .

123

Jack Hayford
© 1981 Rocksmith Music / Leosong Copyright Service Ltd

Majesty – worship his majesty;
unto Jesus be glory,
honour and praise!
Majesty, kingdom, authority,
flow from his throne unto his own:
his anthem raise!

So exalt, lift upon high
the name of Jesus;
magnify, come, glorify
Christ Jesus the king.
Majesty – worship his majesty,
Jesus who died, now glorified,
King of all Kings!

124

Sebastian Temple
© 1967 Franciscan Communications Center

1 Make me a channel of your peace:
where there is hatred let me bring your love,
where there is injury, your pardon, Lord,
and where there's doubt, true faith in you:
O Master, grant
that I may never seek
so much to be consoled
as to console;
to be understood
as to understand,
to be loved,
as to love with all my soul!

2 Make me a channel of your peace:
where there's despair in life let me bring hope,
where there is darkness, only light,
and where there's sadness, ever joy:
O Master, grant . . .

3 Make me a channel of your peace:
it is in pardoning that we are pardoned,
in giving of ourselves that we receive,
and in dying that we're born to eternal life.

* * * *

Make way 1: A Carnival of Praise
Procession songs

125

From Isaiah 61
Graham Kendrick
© 1986 Thankyou Music

1 Make way, make way,
for Christ the king in splendour arrives;
fling wide the gates
and welcome him into your lives.
Make way, make way,
for the King of kings;
make way, make way,
and let his kingdom in!

2 He comes the broken hearts to heal,
the prisoners to free;
the deaf shall hear, the lame shall dance,
the blind shall see.
Make way . . .

3 And those who mourn with heavy hearts,
who weep and sigh,
with laughter, joy and royal crown
he'll beautify.
Make way . . .

4 We call you now to worship him
as Lord of all,
to have no gods before him –
their thrones must fall!
Make way . . .

126

Graham Kendrick
© 1986 Thankyou Music

MEN   We declare
        that the kingdom of God is here,
WOMEN we declare
        that the kingdom of God is here,
MEN   we declare
        that the kingdom of God is here,
WOMEN we declare
        that the kingdom of God is here,
MEN   among you,
WOMEN among you,
MEN   among you,
WOMEN among you.

MEN   We declare . . .

ALL   The blind see, the deaf hear,
     the lame men are walking,
     sicknesses flee at his voice;
     the dead live again
     and the poor hear the good news:
     Jesus is king – so rejoice!

MEN   We declare . . .

ALL   The blind see . . .

MEN   We declare . . .

MEN   We declare
     that the kingdom of God is here,
WOMEN we declare
     that the kingdom of God is here,
MEN   we declare that the
ALL   kingdom of God is here!

127

From Psalm 68
Graham Kendrick
© 1984 Thankyou Music

Let God arise,
and let his enemies be scattered,
and let those who hate him
flee before him;
let God arise,
and let his enemies be scattered,
and let those who hate him
flee away.

MEN
But let the righteous be glad;
let them exult before God,
let them rejoice with gladness,
building up a highway for the king.
We go in the name of the Lord:
let the shout go up in the name of the Lord!

WOMEN
The righteous be glad,
let them exult before God;
O let them rejoice
for the king
in the name of the Lord!

128

Graham Kendrick
© 1986 Thankyou Music

MEN   The earth is the Lord's
WOMEN and everything in it.
MEN   The earth is the Lord's,
WOMEN the work of his hands.
MEN   The earth is the Lord's
WOMEN and everything in it:
ALL   and all things
      were made for his glory!

1 The mountains are his,
  the seas and the islands,
  the cities and towns,
  the houses and streets:
  let rebels bow down
  and worship before him,
  for all things were made for his glory!
     MEN   The earth is the Lord's . . .

2 The mountains are his . . .
     MEN   The earth is the Lord's . . .

MEN   The earth is the Lord's
WOMEN and everything in it.
MEN   The earth is the Lord's,
WOMEN the work of his hands.
MEN   The earth is the Lord's
WOMEN and everything in it:
ALL   and all things were made,
     yes, all things were made,
     and all things were
       made for his glory!

129

Graham Kendrick
© 1986 Thankyou Music

1 We believe in God the Father,
  maker of the universe,
  and in Christ his Son our saviour,
  come to us by Virgin birth.
  We believe he died to save us,
  bore our sins, was crucified;
  then from death he rose victorious,
  ascended to the Father's side.
     Jesus, Lord of all, Lord of all;
     Jesus, Lord of all, Lord of all;
     Jesus, Lord of all, Lord of all;
     Jesus, Lord of all, Lord of all;
     name above all names,
     name above all names!

2 We believe he sends his Spirit
  on his church with gifts of power;
  God, his word of truth affirming,
  sends us to the nations now.
  He will come again in glory,
  judge the living and the dead:
  every knee shall bow before him,
  then must every tongue confess.
     Jesus, Lord of all . . .

     Name above all names!

130
Graham Kendrick
© 1986 Thankyou Music

1 Jesus put this song into our hearts,
  Jesus put this song into our hearts;
  it's a song of joy no-one can take away.
  Jesus put this song into our hearts.

2 Jesus taught us how to live in harmony,
  Jesus taught us how to live in harmony;
  different faces, different races,
        he made us one –
  Jesus taught us how to live in harmony.

3 Jesus taught us how to be a family,
  Jesus taught us how to be a family;
  loving one another with the love that he gives –
  Jesus taught us how to be a family.

4 Jesus turned our sorrow into dancing,
  Jesus turned our sorrow into dancing,
  changed our tears of sadness
        into rivers of joy –
  Jesus turned our sorrows into a dance.

5 *Instrumental*

131
Graham Kendrick
© 1986 Thankyou Music

1 The Lord is marching out in splendour,
  in awesome majesty he rides
  for truth, humility and justice;
  his mighty army fills the skies.
        O give thanks to the Lord
        for his love endures;
        O give thanks to the Lord
        for his love endures;
        O give thanks to the Lord
        for his love endures
        for ever, for ever!

2 His army marches out with dancing,
  for he has filled our hearts with joy:
  be glad the Kingdom is advancing,
  the love of God our battle-cry.
        O give thanks . . .
        O give thanks . . .
        O give thanks . . .
        for ever, for ever,
        for ever!

132
Graham Kendrick
© 1986 Thankyou Music

1 In the tomb so cold they laid him,
  death its victim claimed;
  powers of hell, they could not hold him –
  back to life he came!
      MEN   Christ is risen,
      WOMEN   Christ is risen!
      MEN   Death has been conquered,
      WOMEN   death has been conquered!
      MEN   Christ is risen,
      WOMEN   Christ is risen:
      ALL   he shall reign for ever!

2 Hell has spent its fury on him,
  left him crucified;
  yet by blood he boldly conquered,
  sin and death defied.
      MEN   Christ is risen . . .

3 Now the fear of death is broken,
  Love has won the crown.
  Prisoners of the darkness – listen,
  walls are tumbling down!
      MEN   Christ is risen . . .

4 Raised from death, to heaven ascending,
  Love's exalted king:
  let his song of joy unending
  through the nations ring!
      MEN   Christ is risen . . .

* * * *

133
Luke Connaughton (1917–1979)
© McCrimmon Publishing Co. Ltd

1 Love is his word, love is his way,
  feasting with all, fasting alone,
  living and dying, rising again,
  love, only love, is his way:
      Richer than gold is the love of my Lord,
      better than splendour and wealth.

2 Love is his way, love is his mark,
  sharing his last Passover feast,
  Christ at his table, host to the twelve,
  love, only love, is his mark:
      Richer than gold . . .

3 Love is his mark, love is his sign,
  bread for our strength, wine for our joy,
  'This is my body, this is my blood' –
  love, only love, is his sign:
      Richer than gold . . .

4 Love is his sign, love is his news,
  'Do this,' he said,'lest you forget
  all my deep sorrow, all my dear blood' –
  love, only love, is his news:
      Richer than gold . . .

5 Love is his news, love is his name,
  we are his own, chosen and called,
  family, brethren, cousins and kin,
  love, only love, is his name:
      Richer than gold . . .

6 Love is his name, love is his law,
  hear his command, all who are his:
  'Love one another, I have loved you' –
  love, only love, is his law.
      Richer than gold . . .

7 Love is his law, love is his word:
  love of the Lord, Father and Word,
  love of the Spirit, God ever one,
  love, only love, is his word:
      Richer than gold . . .

134
Graham Kendrick
© 1988 Make Way Music / Thankyou Music

May our worship be acceptable
   in your sight, O Lord;
may our worship be acceptable
   in your sight, O Lord;
may the words of my mouth be pure,
   and the meditation of my heart;
may our worship be acceptable
   in your sight, O Lord.

135
Graham Kendrick
© 1986 Thankyou Music

1 MEN   May the fragrance of Jesus
              fill this place,
  WOMEN may the fragrance of Jesus
              fill this place,
  MEN   may the fragrance of Jesus
              fill this place;
  WOMEN lovely fragrance of Jesus,
  ALL   rising from the sacrifice
              of lives laid down in adoration.

2 MEN   May the glory of Jesus fill his church,
  WOMEN may the glory of Jesus fill his church,
  MEN   may the glory of Jesus fill his church;
  WOMEN radiant glory of Jesus,
  ALL   shining from our faces
              as we gaze in adoration.

3 MEN   May the beauty of Jesus fill my life,
  WOMEN may the beauty of Jesus fill my life,
  MEN   may the beauty of Jesus fill my life:
  WOMEN perfect beauty of Jesus,
  ALL   fill my thoughts, my words, my deeds –
              my all I give in adoration;
              fill my thoughts, my words, my deeds –
              my all I give in adoration.

136
K B Wilkinson (1859–1928)
© in this version Jubilate Hymns †

1 May the mind of Christ my saviour
   live in me from day to day,
   by his love and power controlling
   all I do and say.

2 May the word of God enrich me
   with his truth, from hour to hour;
   so that all may see I triumph
   only through his power.

3 May the peace of God my Father
   in my life for ever reign,
   that I may be calm to comfort
   those in grief and pain.

4 May the love of Jesus fill me
   as the waters fill the sea,
   him exalting, self abasing –
   this is victory!

5 May his beauty rest upon me
   as I seek to make him known;
   so that all may look to Jesus,
   seeing him alone.

137
E Farjeon (1881–1965)
© David Higham Associates Ltd

1 Morning has broken
   like the first morning;
  blackbird has spoken
   like the first bird:
  praise for the singing,
   praise for the morning,
  praise from them springing
   fresh from the word!

2 Sweet the rain's new fall,
   sunlit from heaven,
  like the first dew fall
   on the first grass:
  praise for the sweetness
   of the wet garden,
  sprung in completeness
   where his feet pass.

3 Mine is the sunlight,
   mine is the morning
  born of the one light
   Eden saw play:
  praise with elation,
   praise every morning,
  God's re-creation
   of the new day!

138
Graham Kendrick
© 1986 Thankyou Music

1 Meekness and majesty,
  manhood and deity,
  in perfect harmony –
  the man who is God:
  Lord of eternity
  dwells in humanity,
  kneels in humility
  and washes our feet.
     Oh what a mystery –
     meekness and majesty:
     bow down and worship,
     for this is your God,
     this is your God!

2 Father's pure radiance,
  perfect in innocence,
  yet learns obedience
  to death on a cross:
  suffering to give us life,
  conquering through sacrifice –
  and, as they crucify,
  prays, 'Father, forgive'.
     Oh what a mystery . . .

3 Wisdom unsearchable,
  God the invisible,
  love indestructible
  in frailty appears:
  Lord of infinity,
  stooping so tenderly,
  lifts our humanity
  to the heights of his throne.
     Oh what a mystery . . .

139 © Christopher Idle / Jubilate Hymns †

1 My Lord, you wore no royal crown;
you did not wield the powers of state,
nor did you need a scholar's gown
or priestly robe, to make you great.

2 You never used a killer's sword
to end an unjust tyranny;
your only weapon was your word,
for truth alone could set us free.

3 You did not live a world away
in hermit's cell or desert cave,
but felt our pain and shared each day
with those you came to seek and save.

4 You made no mean or cunning move,
chose no unworthy compromise,
but carved a track of burning love
through tangles of deceit and lies.

5 You came unequalled, undeserved,
to be what we were meant to be:
to serve, instead of being served –
a light for all the world to see.

6 So when I stumble, set me right;
command my life as you require;
let all your gifts be my delight
and you, my Lord, my one desire.

140 © Timothy Dudley-Smith

1 Name of all majesty,
fathomless mystery,
king of the ages
by angels adored;
   power and authority,
   splendour and dignity,
   bow to his mastery –
Jesus is Lord!

2 Child of our destiny,
God from eternity,
love of the Father
on sinners outpoured;
   see now what God has done
   sending his only Son,
   Christ the belovèd One –
Jesus is Lord!

3 Saviour of Calvary,
costliest victory,
darkness defeated
and Eden restored;
   born as a man to die,
   nailed to a cross on high,
   cold in the grave to lie –
Jesus is Lord!

4 Source of all sovereignty,
light, immortality,
life everlasting
and heaven assured;
   so with the ransomed, we
   praise him eternally,
   Christ in his majesty –
Jesus is Lord!

141 © Christopher Idle / Jubilate Hymns †

1 Now let us learn of Christ:
he speaks, and we shall find
he lightens our dark mind;
so let us learn of Christ.

2 Now let us love in Christ
as he has first loved us;
as he endured the cross,
so let us love in Christ.

3 Now let us grow in Christ
and look to things above,
and speak the truth in love;
so let us grow in Christ.

4 Now let us stand in Christ
in every trial we meet,
in all his strength complete;
so let us stand in Christ.

142 © Christopher Walker / Clifton Music

1 No more weeping,
joy has come into the world –
he is risen!

2 Do not fear, Jesus has conquered –
he is risen from the dead!

3 Jesus lives – the Lord of lords
fills the world with his glory;
he has risen from the dead!
In joyfulness we greet the risen Lord,
singing Jesus lives . . .

4 The Lord is calling his disciples
to send us out into the world;
for we love him, we believe him,
and will follow him till we rise with him.
The . . .

5 Sing him praise all of our days –
blessings on him for ever;
sing him praise all of our days,
for his name is Wonderful, Counsellor.
So sing . . .

6 Glory in the highest heaven!

143
Joanne Pond
© 1980 Thankyou Music

O give thanks to the Lord,
all you his people.
O give thanks to the Lord,
for he is good;
let us praise, let us thank,
let us celebrate and dance:
O give thanks to the Lord,
for he is good.

144
Vanessa Strachan
© 1987 'Dont call me Music'

1 O Father, we bless your name
and come now to sing your praises;
O Father, we bless your name
and come now to sing your praises:
we join in with all creation
to worship and honour you,
with thanks that you call us children
and we can be born anew.
Come and sing, come and sing,
come and sing,
come and sing to the Lord your God;
come and sing, come and sing,
come and sing,
come and sing to the Lord your God.

2 Christ Jesus, we love you, Lord,
and long for your kingdom coming;
Christ Jesus, we love you, Lord,
and long for your kingdom coming:
you ask us to love each other
as you here on earth have done –
no status or class or culture
shall keep us from being one.
Come and sing . . .

3 O Spirit, we need your power –
break into our lives and fill us;
O Spirit, we need your power –
break into our lives and fill us:
we long for your signs and wonders
on earth as it is in heaven,
so we can reach out to others –
all glory to you be given!
Come and sing . . .

145
C Wesley (1707–1788)

1 O for a thousand tongues to sing
my great redeemer's praise,
the glories of my God and king,
the triumphs of his grace!

2 Jesus, the name that charms our fears
and bids our sorrows cease –
this music in the sinner's ears
is life and health and peace.

3 He breaks the power of cancelled sin,
he sets the prisoner free;
his blood can make the foulest clean,
his blood availed for me.

4 He speaks – and, listening to his voice,
new life the dead receive,
the mournful broken hearts rejoice,
the humble poor believe.

5 Hear him, you deaf! his praise, you dumb,
your loosened tongues employ;
you blind, now see your saviour come,
and leap, you lame, for joy!

6 My gracious Master and my God,
assist me to proclaim
and spread through all the earth abroad
the honours of your name.

146
Howard Francis and Wayne Wilson
© 1985 Stanmore Music

Oh, isn't it good to be as one,
living in perfect harmony,
sharing the good things God has done,
God has done?

Oh, isn't it good . . .

SOLO VERSE
Oh, isn't it beautiful to be
sharing everything,
the way the Lord wants us to be?
And I feel that we should all be
sharing everything –
together we shall stand!
Oh, isn't it good . . .

147
© Michael Perry / Jubilate Hymns †

1 O God beyond all praising,
we worship you today
and sing the love amazing
that songs cannot repay;
for we can only wonder
at every gift you send,
at blessings without number
and mercies without end:
we lift our hearts before you
and wait upon your word,
we honour and adore you,
our great and mighty Lord.

2 Then hear, O gracious Saviour,
accept the love we bring,
that we who know your favour
may serve you as our king;
and whether our tomorrows
be filled with good or ill,
we'll triumph through our sorrows
and rise to bless you still:
to marvel at your beauty
and glory in your ways,
and make a joyful duty
our sacrifice of praise!

148

Patrick Appleford
© 1965 Josef Weinberger Ltd

1 O Lord, all the world belongs to you,
and you are always making all things new.
What is wrong you forgive;
and the new life you give
is what's turning the world upside down.

2 The world's only loving to its friends,
but your way of loving never ends –
loving enemies too.
And this loving with you
is what's turning the world upside down.

3 The world lives divided and apart;
you draw us together, and we start
in our friendship to see
that in harmony we
can be turning the world upside down.

4 The world wants the wealth to live in state,
but you show a new way to be great:
like a servant you came
and, if we do the same,
we'll be turning the world upside down.

5 O Lord, all the world belongs to you,
and you are always making all things new.
What is wrong you forgive;
and the new life you give
is what's turning the world upside down.

148A   PRAISE SHOUT
From Psalms 82, 83

LEADER Come, O God, and rule the earth:
ALL **all the nations are yours!**

LEADER Let them know that you are king,
ALL **sovereign over all the world! Amen.**

149

Jacques Berthier
© Taizé. Used by permission of Wm Collins

O Lord, hear my prayer;
O Lord, hear my prayer:
when I call, answer me –
O Lord, hear my prayer;
O Lord, hear my prayer;
come and listen to me.

O Lord . . .

150

Michael Smith
© 1981 Meadowgreen Music /
Tree Publishing Co. Inc.

O Lord, our Lord,
how majestic is your name in all the earth;
O Lord, our Lord,
how majestic is your name in all the earth;
O Lord, we praise your name;
O Lord, we magnify your name.

Prince of peace, mighty God,
O Lord God almighty!

151

Graham Kendrick
© 1987 Make Way Music / Thankyou Music

1 O Lord, the clouds are gathering,
the fire of judgement burns.
How we have fallen!
O Lord, you stand appalled to see
your laws of love so scorned.
and lives so broken.

MEN Have mercy, Lord,
WOMEN have mercy, Lord.
MEN Forgive us, Lord,
WOMEN forgive us, Lord.
ALL Restore us, Lord;
revive your church again.
MEN Let justice flow,
WOMEN let justice flow,
MEN like rivers,
WOMEN like rivers;
ALL and righteousness
like a never-failing stream.

2 O Lord, over the nations now,
where is the dove of peace?
Her wings are broken,
O Lord, while precious children starve,
the tools of war increase,
their bread is stolen.

MEN Have mercy, Lord . . .

3 O Lord, dark powers are poised
to flood our streets with hate and fear.
We must awaken!
O Lord, let love reclaim the lives
that sin would sweep away,
and let your kingdom come!

MEN Have mercy, Lord . . .

4 Yet, O Lord, your glorious cross
shall tower triumphant in this land,
evil confounding;
through the fire, your suffering church
display the glories of her Christ,
praises resounding.

MEN Have mercy, Lord . . .

A never-failing stream.

152

Graham Kendrick
© 1986 Thankyou Music

O Lord, your tenderness –
melting all my bitterness!
O Lord, I receive your love.
O Lord, your loveliness,
changing all my ugliness,
O Lord, I receive your love;
O Lord, I receive your love;
O Lord, I receive your love.

153

From Psalm 117
Jaqcues Berthier
© Taizé. Used by permission of Wm Collins

CONTINUOUS RESPONSE

O praise the Lord our God,
O praise the Lord our God,
all you people – Alleluia!

O praise . . .

Laudate Dominum,
laudate Dominum
omnes gentes – alleluia!

SOLO VERSES

1 Praise the Lord, all you nations,
praise him, all you peoples –
Alleluia.

2 Strong is his love and mercy,
he is faithful for ever –
Alleluia!

3 Alleluia, alleluia –
let everything living
give praise to the Lord!

4 Alleluia, alleluia . . .

154

From Psalm 100
in *The Psalms, A New Translation for Worship*
© 1976, 1977 David Frost,
John Emerton and Andrew Macintosh

^AO shout to the Lord in triumph
all the earth,
^BO shout to the Lord in triumph
all the earth;
^AServe the Lord with gladness,
^Bserve the Lord with gladness,
^Aand come before his face
with songs of joy,
^Band come before his face
with songs of joy!

^AO shout to the Lord . . .

1 ALL Know that the Lord, he is God;
it is he who has made us and we are his:
we are his people
and the sheep of his pasture.

^ACome into his gates with thanksgiving,
^Bcome into his gates with thanksgiving,
^Aand into his courts with praise,
^Band into his courts with praise;
^Agive thanks to him
and bless his holy name,
^Bgive thanks to him
and bless his holy name.

2 ALL For the Lord, the Lord is good:
his loving mercy is for ever,
his faithfulness
throughout all generations.

^AO shout to the Lord . . .

^ACome into his gates . . .

(The singers divide at A and B)

155

From Psalm 104
after W Kethe (died 1594)
R Grant (1779–1838)

1 O worship the King
all glorious above,
and gratefully sing
his power and his love,
our shield and defender,
the Ancient of Days,
pavilioned in splendour
and girded with praise.

2 O tell of his might
and sing of his grace,
whose robe is the light,
whose canopy space;
his chariots of wrath
the deep thunder-clouds form,
and dark is his path
on the wings of the storm.

3 The earth, with its store
of wonders untold,
Almighty, your power
has founded of old,
established it fast
by a changeless decree,
and round it has cast
like a mantle the sea.

4 Your bountiful care
what tongue can recite?
It breathes in the air,
it shines in the light,
it streams from the hills,
it descends to the plain,
and sweetly distils
in the dew and the rain.

5 We children of dust
are feeble and frail –
in you we will trust,
for you never fail;
your mercies how tender,
how firm to the end,
our maker, defender,
redeemer and friend!

6 O measureless Might,
unchangeable Love,
whom angels delight
to worship above:
your ransomed creation
with glory ablaze,
in true adoration
shall sing to your praise!

156

African origin edited by Anders Nyberg
© Wild Goose Publications / The Iona Community

1 Oh freedom (freedom is coming),
   oh freedom (freedom is coming),
   oh freedom (freedom is coming –
      Oh yes I know)!

   Oh freedom . . .

   Oh yes, I know (oh yes I know),
   oh yes, I know (oh yes I know),
   oh yes, I know (oh yes I know,
      oh yes I know):

   Oh yes, I know . . .

2 Oh Jesus (Jesus is coming),
   oh Jesus, (Jesus is coming),
   oh Jesus (Jesus is coming –
      oh yes, I know)!

   Oh Jesus . . .

   Oh yes, I know (oh yes I know),
   oh yes, I know (oh yes I know),
   oh yes, I know (oh yes I know,
      oh yes I know):

   Oh yes I know . . .

157

African origin edited by Anders Nyberg
© Wild Goose Publications / The Iona Community

1 On earth an army is marching:
   we're going home,
   our longing bears a song,
   so sing out strong.
   On earth an army . . .
      Singing (Alleluia),
      singing (Alleluia),
      singing Alleluia,
      alleluia, alleluia!
      Singing (Alleluia), . . .

2 With love our hearts are ablazing
   for those who roam
   and wander far away,
   yet long for home.
   With love . . .
      Singing (Alleluia) . . .

3 Each day our friendship is growing,
   and with all speed;
   we share our wine and bread,
   a hasty meal.
   Each day . . .
      Singing (Alleluia) . . .

AFRICAN VERSE

*Singabahambayo thina
kulomhlaba
kepha sinekhaya
eZulwini.
Singabahambayo . . .
   Sithi (haleluya),
   sithi (haleluya),
   sithi haleluya,
   haleluya, haleluya!
   Sithi (haleluya) . . .*

158

Robert Cull
© 1976 Maranatha! Music / Word Music (UK)

Open our eyes, Lord,
   we want to see Jesus –
to reach out and touch him
   and say that we love him;
open our ears, Lord,
   and help us to listen:
O open our eyes, Lord,
   we want to see Jesus!

159

Carl Tuttle
© 1982 Mercy Publishing / Thankyou Music

Open your eyes,
see the glory of the King;
lift up your voice,
and his praises sing!

   I love you, Lord,
   I will proclaim:
   Alleluia!
   I bless your name.

160

Lance Lincoln
© Copyright controlled

Praise and adoration!
I sing an acclamation
all for the exaltation of the King:
I love a celebration and loud jubilation;
it stirs anticipation of your return.
   Let us sing out to the King,
   let us sing out to the King!

161

From Psalm 150
John Kennett
© 1981 Thankyou Music

Praise him on the trumpet,
      the psaltery and harp;
praise him on the timbrel and the dance;
praise him with stringed instruments too;
praise him on the loud cymbals,
praise him on the loud cymbals:
let everything that has breath praise the Lord!

Alleluia – praise the Lord;
alleluia – praise the Lord:
let everything that has breath praise the Lord!

Alleluia . . .

162

From Psalm 148
Bill Batstone and Tom Howard
© 1982 Maranatha! Music / Word Music (UK)

Praise the Lord,
praise the Lord from the heavens;
all the angels sing: Praise the Lord!
Praise the Lord –
from the heights of creation
they shall praise the name of the Lord.

1 He commanded them
and the heavens were made,
he established them
and they won't pass away:
the sun and moon
praise the Lord with their light;
all the stars up above,
they keep shining through the night.
Praise the Lord . . .

2 And on the earth
let all nature agree –
from the mountain-tops
to the depths of the sea:
the winds and rain
and the fiery light,
all the beasts of the field,
all the birds in their flight.
Praise the Lord . . .

3 All the people
who inhabit the world,
from the ruling kings
to the boys and the girls;
the young and old
join in praise to his name:
God alone is supreme
let creation proclaim!
Praise the Lord . . .

163

From Psalm 103
H F Lyte (1793–1847)

1 Praise, my soul, the king of heaven!
to his feet your tribute bring:
ransomed, healed, restored, forgiven,
who like me his praise should sing?
Alleluia, alleluia!
praise the everlasting king!

2 Praise him for his grace and favour
to his people in distress;
praise him still the same as ever,
slow to blame and swift to bless:
Alleluia, alleluia!
glorious in his faithfulness!

3 Father-like, he tends and spares us;
all our hopes and fears he knows,
in his hands he gently bears us,
rescues us from all our foes,
Alleluia, alleluia!
widely as his mercy flows.

4 Angels, help us to adore him –
you behold him face to face;
sun and moon, bow down before him –
praise him, all in time and space:
Alleluia, alleluia!
praise with us the God of grace!

164

African origin edited by Anders Nyberg
© Wild Goose Publications / The Iona Community

Praise the Father,
liberator, Lord;
praise the Father,
liberator, Lord!
He frees all the captives
and gives the hungry bread;
he frees all the captives
and gives the hungry bread.

Praise the Father . . .

AFRICAN VERSE

Gabi, Gabi,
bash' abazalwan'.
Gabi, Gabi,
bash' abazalwan'.
Siyoshiywa khona,
sidal' ubuzalwan'.
Siyoshiywa khona,
sidal' ubuzalwan'.

Gabi, Gabi . . .

164A PRAISE SHOUT

From Psalm 107

LEADER Let us give thanks to the Lord
for his unfailing love
ALL **and the wonders he has done for us.**

LEADER He satisfies the thirsty
ALL **and fills the hungry with good things.**

165

Graham Kendrick
© 1984 Thankyou Music

1 Praise to the Lord!
Sing alleluias to the king of all the earth.
Praise to his name!
Let every creature join in the joyful song.
MEN I will praise him,
WOMEN I will praise him;
MEN I will exalt him,
WOMEN I will exalt him –
MEN for his love,
WOMEN for his love,
ALL for his love endures for ever.

2 Praise to the Lord!
The wind and the waves,
the thunder and rain,
display his power:
raise now the shout;
come, lift up your voice
and join with all nature's song.
MEN I will praise him . . .

3 Praise to the Lord!
O taste and see
his goodness and mercy
never fail.
Praise to his name,
who gives to his children
gifts from his generous hand.
      MEN   I will praise him . . .

166
Jennifer Randolph
© 1985 Hosanna! Music / Frontier Music

Prince of peace, counsellor,
merciful Son of God;
Lord of hosts, (Lord of hosts),
conqueror, (conqueror),
coming king, and ever-living God!
I extol you, Lord, I extol you:
you are high above the earth
all creation shouts your worth –
I extol you, Lord, I extol you,
my Jehovah, I extol you.

167
Graham Kendrick
© 1988 Make Way Music / Thankyou Music

1   LEADER Raise the shout:
      ALL   Jesus reigns!
      LEADER Shout it out:
      ALL   Jesus reigns!
Christ the fight did win,
smashed the power of sin,
love has broken in among us.

2   LEADER Raise the shout:
      ALL   Jesus lives!
      LEADER Shout it out:
      ALL   Jesus lives!
He burst from the grave,
now has power to save
all who put their trust in him.

168
Dave Bilbrough
© 1984 Thankyou Music

Reigning in all splendour –
victorious love;
Christ Jesus the saviour,
transcendent above.
All earthly dominions
and kingdoms shall fall,
for his name is Jesus
and he is the Lord.
    He is Lord,
    he is Lord,
    he is Lord,
    he is Lord.

169
Graham Kendrick
© 1983 Thankyou Music

Rejoice, rejoice! Christ is in you –
the hope of glory in our hearts.
He lives, he lives!
his breath is in you.
Arise! A mighty army we arise!

1 Now is the time for us to march upon the land –
into our hands he will give the ground we claim;
he rides in majesty to lead us into victory,
the world shall see that Christ is Lord.
    Rejoice . . .

2 God is at work in us his purpose to perform –
building a kingdom of power not of words;
where things impossible
    by faith shall be made possible:
let's give the glory to him now.
    Rejoice . . .

3 Though we are weak,
    his grace is everything we need –
we're made of clay, but this treasure is within;
he turns our weaknesses into his opportunities,
so that the glory goes to him.
    Rejoice . . .

170
Chris Bowater
© 1986 Word Music (UK)

Rejoice, rejoice, rejoice,
rejoice, rejoice, rejoice;
my soul rejoices in the Lord.
    Rejoice . . .

My soul magnifies the Lord,
and my spirit rejoices in God my saviour;
my soul magnifies the Lord,
and my spirit rejoices in my God.
    Rejoice . . .

171
From Psalm 25
Verses: © The Grail / A P Watt Ltd
Chorus: © Paul Inwood / Magnificat Music

    ALL Remember, remember your mercy, Lord;
remember, remember your mercy, Lord:
hear your people's prayer
    as they call to you;
remember, remember your mercy, Lord.

1 SOLO
Lord, make me know your ways,
Lord, teach me your paths;
make me walk in your truth, and teach me,
for you are God my saviour.
    ALL Remember, remember your mercy . . .

2 SOLO
Remember your mercy, Lord,
and the love you have shown from of old;
do not remember the sins of my youth.
    In your love remember me,
    in your love remember me
because of your goodness, O Lord.
    ALL Remember, remember your mercy . . .

3 SOLO
The Lord is good and upright,
he shows the path to all who stray;
he guides the humble in the right path,
he teaches his way to the poor.
    ALL Remember, remember your mercy . . .

172
Graham Kendrick and Chris Rolinson
© 1981 Thankyou Music

1 Restore, O Lord,
   the honour of your name!
   In works of sovereign power
   come shake the earth again,
   that all may see,
   and come with reverent fear
   to the living God
   whose Kingdom shall outlast the years.

2 Restore, O Lord,
   in all the earth your fame,
   and in our time revive
   the Church that bears your name;
   and in your anger,
   Lord, remember mercy –
   O living God,
   whose mercy shall outlast the years.

3 Bend us, O Lord,
   where we are hard and cold,
   in your refiner's fire;
   come purify the gold:
   though suffering comes,
   and evil crouches near,
   still our living God
   is reigning – he is reigning here!

4 Restore, O Lord,
   the honour of your name!
   In works of sovereign power
   come shake the earth again,
   that all may see,
   and come with reverent fear
   to the living God
   whose Kingdom shall outlast the years.

173
© David Mowbray / Jubilee Hymns †

1 Risen Lord, whose name we cherish,
   all the stars are in your hand!
   Walk today among your people,
   light each candle on its stand;
   look in mercy, not in judgement,
   on your church in every land.

2 For, divided in your service,
   we have chosen selfish ways,
   lived in bitterness of spirit,
   quickly let our anger blaze;
   often blindly followed leaders,
   sought our glory, not your praise.

3 Yet your church has also triumphed,
   told of love's great offering,
   in its life shown forth your goodness,
   drawn from death its cruel sting;
   wakened to the needs of many,
   soothed the sorrows life can bring.

4 So, we pray, that by your Spirit
   all your scattered flock may find
   that deep unity you prayed for
   and would share with all mankind;
   by this gift our fears and envies
   shall in truth be left behind.

5 Risen Lord, your hand is knocking
   at each church's bolted door!
   Enter now, and dwell within us,
   trust and fellowship restore;
   that your Father's joys together
   all may taste for evermore.

174
Douglas Brown
© 1980 Thankyou Music

1 River, wash over me,
   cleanse me and make me new;
   bathe me, refresh me and fill me anew –
   river, wash over me.

2 Spirit, watch over me,
   lead me to Jesus' feet;
   cause me to worship and fill me anew –
   Spirit, watch over me.

3 Jesus, rule over me,
   reign over all my heart;
   teach me to praise you and fill me anew –
   Jesus, rule over me.

175
Chris Bowater
© 1985 Word Music (UK)

Reign in me, sovereign Lord, reign in me,
reign in me, sovereign Lord, reign in me.
   Captivate my heart,
   let your kingdom come,
   establish there your throne,
   let your will be done!

Reign in me . . .

176
John Pantry
© 1986 Ears and Eyes Music

Send me out from here Lord,
to serve a world in need;
may I know no-one
   by the coat they wear,
but the heart that Jesus sees.
And may the light of your face
shine upon me Lord –
You have filled my heart
   with the greatest joy
and my cup is overflowing.

1 'Go now, and carry the news to all creation –
   every race and every tongue;
   take no purse with you, take nothing to eat
   for he will supply your every need.'
      Send me out . . .

2 'Go now, bearing the light, living for others,
fearlessly walking into the night;
take no thought for your lives –
like lambs among wolves –
full of the Spirit, ready to die.'
Send me out . . .
. . . and my cup
is overflowing with joy!

177

African origin edited by Anders Nyberg
© Wild Goose Publications / The Iona Community

1 LEADER Send me, Lord:
ALL   Send me, Jesus
send me, Jesus
send me, Jesus
send me, Lord.

2 LEADER Lead me, Lord:
ALL   Lead me, Jesus . . .

3 LEADER Fill me, Lord:
ALL   Fill me, Jesus . . .

AFRICAN VERSE

Thuma mina,
thuma mina
thuma mina
thuma mina,
Somandla.

178

Graham Kendrick
© 1988 Make Way Music / Thankyou Music

Send, send more labourers
to the harvest fields;
send, send more labourers,
that your love may be revealed,
that your name
may be known in all the earth –
Jesus' fame,
far and wide in all the earth:
Lord of the harvest,
Lord of the harvest, we cry to you:

179

From Psalm 100
John Daniels
© 1986 Word Music (UK)

1 Shout for joy and sing,
serve the Lord your king,
coming before him
joyfully – and sing,
knowing that the Lord is God;
he has made us, we are his –
in his pasture we have food
and in his presence live (evermore).
Shout for joy . . .

2 Enter in his gates
and his courts with praise,
giving thanks to him
throughout all our days:
for the Lord our God is good,
and his love has ever stood;
faithfully he keeps his word;
and his love to all (generations).
Enter in his gates . . .

180

Tom Brooks
© 1985 Hosanna! Music / Frontier Music

Shout! Shout joyfully to your God, all the earth!
Shout! Shout joyfully to your God, all the earth!
Sing the glory of his name
and make his praises glorious.
Shout! Shout joyfully to your God, all the earth!
Shout . . .

Joyfully, joyfully,
all the earth shall bow the knee;
joyfully, joyfully,
we will sing in harmony,
singing praises to your name!
Shout . . .

181

Graham Kendrick
© 1988 Make Way Music / Thankyou Music

1 Show your power, O Lord,
demonstrate the justice of your kingdom;
prove your mighty word,
vindicate your name
before a watching world.
Awesome are your deeds, O Lord –
renew them for this hour.
Show your power, O Lord –
among the people now.

2 Show your power, O Lord,
cause your church to rise and take action;
let all fear be gone,
powers of the age to come
are breaking through.
We your people are ready to serve,
to arise and to obey.
Show your power, O Lord,
and set the people –
show your power, O Lord,
and set the people –
show your power, O Lord,
and set the people free!

182

Verse 1 © 1974 Linda Stassen / New Song Ministries
verses 2–4 anonymous

1 Sing alleluia to the Lord,
sing alleluia to the Lord,
sing alleluia, sing alleluia,
sing alleluia to the Lord!

2 Jesus is risen from the dead,
Jesus is risen from the dead,
Jesus is risen, Jesus is risen,
Jesus is risen from the dead!

3 Jesus is Lord of heaven and earth,
Jesus is Lord of heaven and earth,
Jesus is Lord, Jesus is Lord,
Jesus is Lord of heaven and earth!

4 Jesus is coming for his own,
Jesus is coming for his own,
Jesus is coming, Jesus is coming,
Jesus is coming for his own.

183

1 Sing of the Lord's goodness,
Father of all wisdom,
come to him and bless his name.
Mercy he has shown us,
his love is for ever,
faithful to the end of days.
    Come then all you nations,
    sing of your Lord's goodness,
    melodies of praise and thanks to God;
    ring out the Lord's glory,
    praise him with your music,
    worship him and bless his name.

2 Power he has wielded,
honour is his garment,
risen from the snares of death.
His word he has spoken,
one bread he has broken,
new life he now gives to all.
    Come then . . .

3 Courage in our darkness,
comfort in our sorrow –
Spirit of our God most high!
Solace for the weary,
pardon for the sinner,
splendour of the living God!
    Come then . . .

4 Praise him with your singing,
praise him with the trumpet,
praise God with the lute and harp.
Praise him with the cymbals,
praise him with your dancing,
praise God till the end of days.
    Come then . . .

184

1 Sing praise to the Lord!
    praise him in the height;
rejoice in his word
    you angels of light:
you heavens, adore him
    by whom you were made,
and worship before him
    in brightness arrayed.

2 Sing praise to the Lord!
    praise him upon earth
in tuneful accord,
    you saints of new birth:
praise him who has brought you
    his grace from above;
praise him who has taught you
    to sing of his love.

3 Sing praise to the Lord!
    all things that give sound,
each jubilant chord
    re-echo around:

loud organs, his glory
    proclaim in deep tone,
and sweet harp, the story
    of what he has done.

4 Sing praise to the Lord!
    thanksgiving and song
to him be outpoured
    all ages along;
for love in creation,
    for heaven restored,
for grace of salvation,
    sing praise to the Lord!

185

1 Sing to the Lord
    with a song of profound delight,
serve him by day
    and bring praises in the night:
MEN   tell of the battles fought for us,
ALL – 1   marvellous,
ALL – 2   glorious;
WOMEN   tell of his wonders done for us,
ALL   worthy of acclaim . . .

2 Beauty and power
    are the marks of our Saviour's grace,
splendour and light
    shine in glory from his face:
MEN   worship the Lord in holiness,
ALL – 1   faithfulness,
ALL – 2   godliness –
WOMEN   judging the world with righteousness
ALL   he will come to reign . . .

3 So let the skies sing aloud
    and the earth rejoice –
beasts of the field
    and the forest lift their voice:
MEN   firmly he set the solid ground,
ALL – 1   seas abound,
ALL – 2   skies resound;
WOMEN   all we desire in God is found –
ALL   glory to his name!

186

1 Sing to the world of Christ our sovereign Lord,
tell of his birth which brought new life to all;
speak of his life, his love, his holy word,
let every nation hear and know his call:
sing to the world of Christ our sovereign Lord.

2 Sing to the world of Christ the Prince of peace
showing to us the Father's loving care,
pleading that love should reign
        that wars might cease,
teaching we need the love of God to share:
sing to the world of Christ the Prince of peace.

3 Sing to the world of Christ our steadfast friend
offering himself to live the constant sign,
food for our souls until we meet life's end –
gives us his flesh for bread, his blood for wine
sing to the world of Christ our steadfast friend.

4 Sing to the world of Christ our saviour king,
   born that his death
              the world's release should win:
   hung on a cross, forgiveness he could bring,
   buried, he rose to conquer death and sin –
   sing to the world of Christ our Saviour king.

5 Sing to the world of Christ at God's right hand:
   praise to the Spirit both have sent from heaven,
   living in us till earth shall reach its span,
   time be no more, and Christ shall come again:
   sing to the world of Christ at God's right hand.

187
From Psalm 98
© Michael Baughen / Jubilate Hymns †

1 Sing to God new songs of worship –
   all his deeds are marvellous;
   he has brought salvation to us
   with his hand and holy arm:
   he has shown to all the nations
   righteousness and saving power;
   he recalled his truth and mercy
   to his people Israel.

2 Sing to God new songs of worship –
   earth has seen his victory;
   let the lands of earth be joyful
   praising him with thankfulness:
   sound upon the harp his praises,
   play to him with melody;
   let the trumpets sound his triumph,
   show your joy to God the king!

3 Sing to God new songs of worship –
   let the sea now make a noise;
   all on earth and in the waters
   sound your praises to the Lord:
   let the hills rejoice together,
   let the rivers clap their hands,
   for with righteousness and justice
   he will come to judge the earth.

188
Graham Kendrick
© 1988 Make Way Music / Thankyou Music

Soften my heart, Lord,
soften my heart;
from all indifference
set me apart
to feel your compassion,
to weep with your tears –
come soften my heart,
O Lord, soften my heart.

189
David Bilbrough
© 1983 Thankyou Music

1 So freely
   flows the endless love you give to me;
   so freely,
   not dependent on my part.
   As I am reaching out,
   reveal the love within your heart;
   as I am reaching out,
   reveal the love within your heart!

2 Completely –
   that's the way you give your love to me,
   completely,
   not dependent on my part.
   As I am reaching out,
   reveal the love within your heart;
   as I am reaching out,
   reveal the love within your heart!

3 So easy,
   I receive the love you give to me;
   so easy,
   not dependent on my part.
   Flowing out to me –
   the love within your heart;
   flowing out to me –
   the love within your heart!

190
Andrae Crouch
© 1976 Lexicon Music Incorporated /
Crouch Music (USA)

1 Soon – and very soon –
   we are going to see the King *
       Alleluia, alleluia,
       we're going to see the King!

2 No more crying there . . . *
   Alleluia . . .

3 No more dying there . . . *
   Alleluia . . .

   Alleluia, alleluia, alleluia, alleluia!

4 Soon and very soon . . . *
   Alleluia . . .

   Alleluia, alleluia, alleluia, alleluia!

* These sentences are twice repeated.

191
Chris Bowater
© 1978 Springtide / Word Music (UK)

Spirit of God, show me Jesus;
remove the darkness,
let truth shine through.
Spirit of God, show me Jesus;
reveal the fullness of his love to me!

192
Graham Kendrick
© 1988 Make Way Music / Thankyou Music

1 Such love, pure as the whitest snow,
   such love weeps for the shame I know,
   such love, paying the debt I owe –
       O Jesus, such love!

2 Such love, stilling my restlessness,
   such love, filling my emptiness,
   such love, showing me holiness –
       O Jesus, such love!

3 Such love springs from eternity,
   such love, streaming through history,
   such love, fountain of life to me:
       O Jesus, such love!

193

F R Havergal (1836–1879)
© in this version Jubilate Hymns †

1 Take my life and let it be
all you purpose, Lord, for me;
consecrate my passing days,
let them flow in ceaseless praise.

2 Take my hands, and let them move
at the impulse of your love;
take my feet, and let them run
with the news of victory won.

3 Take my voice, and let me sing
always, only, for my King;
take my lips, let me proclaim
all the beauty of your name.

4 Take my wealth – all I possess,
make me rich in faithfulness;
take my mind that I may use
every power as you shall choose.

5 Take my motives and my will,
all your purpose to fulfil;
take my heart – it is your own,
it shall be your royal throne.

6 Take my love – my Lord, I pour
at your feet its treasure-store;
take myself, and I will be
yours for all eternity.

194

Bryn Rees (1911–1983)
© Mrs M Rees

1 The Kingdom of God
is justice and joy;
for Jesus restores
what sin would destroy.
God's power and glory
in Jesus we know;
and here and hereafter
the kingdom shall grow.

2 The kingdom of God
is mercy and grace;
the captives are freed,
the sinners find place,
the outcast are welcomed
God's banquet to share;
and hope is awakened
in place of despair.

3 The kingdom of God
is challenge and choice:
believe the good news,
repent and rejoice!
His love for us sinners
brought Christ to his cross:
our crisis of judgement
for gain or for loss.

4 God's kingdom is come,
the gift and the goal;
in Jesus begun,
in heaven made whole.
The heirs of the kingdom
shall answer his call;
and all things cry 'Glory!'
to God all in all.

195

John Daniels
© 1986 Thankyou Music

Teach me your way, O Lord,
and I will walk in your truth;
give me an undivided heart
that I may fear your name.

And I will praise you, O Lord my God,
with all of my heart;
and I will praise you, O Lord my God,
and I will glorify your name for ever.

Teach me your way . . .

196

J E Seddon (1915–1983)
© Mrs M Seddon / Jubilate Hymns †

1 Tell all the world of Jesus,
our saviour, Lord and king;
and let the whole creation
of his salvation sing:
proclaim his glorious greatness
in nature and in grace;
creator and redeemer,
the Lord of time and space.

2 Tell all the world of Jesus,
that everyone may find
the joy of his forgiveness –
true peace of heart and mind:
proclaim his perfect goodness,
his deep, unfailing care;
his love so rich in mercy,
a love beyond compare.

3 Tell all the world of Jesus,
that everyone may know
of his almighty triumph
defeating every foe:
proclaim his coming glory,
when sin is overthrown,
and he shall reign in splendour –
the King upon his throne!

197

© Timothy Dudley-Smith

1 Tell out, my soul, the greatness of the Lord!
unnumbered blessings give my spirit voice;
tender to me the promise of his word;
in God my saviour shall my heart rejoice.

2 Tell out, my soul, the greatness of his name!
make known his might,
the deeds his arm has done;
his mercy sure, from age to age the same;
his holy name – the Lord, the mighty one.

3 Tell out, my soul, the greatness of his might!
   powers and dominions lay their glory by.
   Proud hearts and stubborn wills are put to flight,
   the hungry fed, the humble lifted high.

4 Tell out, my soul, the glories of his word!
   firm is his promise, and his mercy sure.
   Tell out, my soul, the greatness of the Lord
   to children's children and for evermore!

198
John Daniels and Phil Thomson
© Ears and Eyes Music

1 The earth was dark until you spoke –
   then all was light and all was peace;
   yet still, O God, so many wait
   to see the flame of love released.
       Lights to the world!
       O Light divine,
       kindle in us a mighty flame,
       till every heart, consumed by love
       shall rise to praise
       your holy name!

2 In Christ you gave your gift of life
   to save us from the depth of night:
   O come and set our spirits free
   and draw us to your perfect light!
       Lights to the world . . .

3 Where there is fear may we bring joy
   and healing to a world in pain:
   Lord, build your kingdom through our lives
   till Jesus walks this earth again.
       Lights to the world . . .

4 O burn in us, that we may burn
   with love that triumphs in despair;
   and touch our lives with such a fire
   that souls may search and find you there.
       Lights to the world . . .

199
Graham Kendrick
© 1981 Thankyou Music

1 The King is among us,
       his Spirit is here:
   let's draw near and worship,
       let songs fill the air!

2 He looks down upon us,
       delight in his face,
   enjoying his children's love,
       enthralled by our praise.

3 For each child is special,
       accepted and loved –
   a love-gift from Jesus
       to his Father above.

4 And now he is giving
       his gifts to us all;
   for no-one is worthless
       and each one is called.

5 The Spirit's anointing
       on all flesh comes down,
   and we shall be channels
       for works like his own:

6 We come now believing
       your promise of power,
   for we are your people
       and this is your hour.

7 The King is among us,
       his Spirit is here:
   let's draw near and worship,
       let songs fill the air!

199A
PRAISE SHOUT
From Psalm 150

LEADER Praise God in his sanctuary;
ALL **praise him in his mighty heavens.**

LEADER Praise him for his acts of power;
ALL **praise him for his surpassing greatness**

LEADER Let everything that has breath
          praise the Lord:
ALL **praise the Lord! Amen!**

200
Chris Bowater
© 1982 Word Music (UK)

The Lord has led forth his people with joy,
and his chosen ones with singing, singing;
the Lord has led forth his people with joy,
and his chosen ones with singing.

He has given to them the lands of the nations,
to possess the fruit and keep his laws,
and praise, praise his name.
   The Lord has led forth . . .

201
Graham Kendrick
© 1988 Make Way Music / Thankyou Music

1 MEN The Lord is a mighty king,
  WOMEN the maker of everything,
  MEN the Lord, he made the earth;
  WOMEN he spoke, and it came at once to birth.
  MEN He said, 'Let us make mankind' –
  WOMEN 'the crown of his design.' –
  MEN 'in our own likeness.'
  WOMEN his image in every human face!

  ALL And he made us for his delight,
          gave us the gift of life,
          created us family,
          to be his glory,
          to be his glory.

2 MEN And yet we were deceived,
  WOMEN in pride the lie believed;
  MEN to sin and death's decay
  WOMEN the whole creation fell that day.
  MEN Now all creation
  WOMEN yearns for liberation –
  MEN all things in Christ restored –
  WOMEN the purchase of his precious blood.
  ALL And he made us . . .

  ALL And he made us . . .

202
Vanessa Strachan
© 1987 'Don't call me Music'

1 The Lord was born a babe in a stable,
poor and bare he died on a tree;
but by the power of love he was able
from the power of death to be free.
   Our Lord, he is the redeemer,
   Jesus Christ – we worship his name:
   so come, believe in his word,
   and you will not be searching again!

2 He healed the sick – it wasn't expected
that our God would stand with the weak –
befriended those that others rejected:
may we too be humble and meek.
   Our Lord . . .

3 It's not by what you do or you don't do
that you are accepted and loved;
but by the grace of God, for he wants to
be your friend in heaven above.
   Our Lord . . .

4 We give back lives and gifts as we bring them –
may we share your love and your word!
And as we see the signs of your kingdom,
we proclaim that 'Yes, you are Lord!'
   Our Lord . . .

203
From Psalm 23
© Christopher Idle / Jubilate Hymns †

1 The Lord my shepherd rules my life
and gives me all I need:
he leads me by refreshing streams;
in pastures green I feed.

2 The Lord revives my failing strength,
he makes my joy complete,
and in right paths, for his name's sake,
he guides my faltering feet.

3 Though in a valley dark as death,
no evil makes me fear,
your shepherd's staff protects my way,
for you are with me there.

4 While all my enemies look on
you spread a royal feast;
you fill my cup, anoint my head,
and treat me as your guest.

5 Your goodness and your gracious love
pursue me all my days;
your house, O Lord, shall be my home –
your name, my endless praise.

6 To Father, Son, and Spirit, praise!
to God whom we adore
be worship, glory, power and love
both now and evermore.

204
C F Alexander (1818–1895)

1 There is a green hill far away,
outside a city wall,
where our dear Lord was crucified,
who died to save us all.

2 We may not know, we cannot tell
what pains he had to bear,
but we believe it was for us
he hung and suffered there.

3 He died that we may be forgiven,
he died to make us good;
that we might go at last to heaven,
saved by his precious blood.

4 There was no other good enough
to pay the price of sin;
he, only, could unlock the gate
of heaven – and let us in.

5 Lord Jesus, dearly you have loved;
and we must love you too,
and trust in your redeeming blood
and learn to follow you.

205
Chris Bowater
© 1985 Word Music (UK)

1 The Spirit of the Lord,
the sovereign Lord, is on me
because he has anointed me
to preach good news to the poor:
   Proclaiming Jesus, only Jesus –
   it is Jesus, saviour, healer and baptizer,
   and the mighty king,
   the victor and deliverer –
   he is Lord, he is Lord, he is Lord!

2 And he has called on me
to bind up all the broken hearts,
to minister release
to every captivated soul:
   Proclaiming Jesus . . .

3 Let righteousness arise
and blossom as a garden;
let praise begin to spring
in every tongue and nation:
   Proclaiming Jesus . . .

206
Graham Kendrick
© 1984 Thankyou Music

1 The price is paid: come, let us enter in
to all that Jesus died to make our own.
For every sin more than enough he gave,
and bought our freedom from each guilty stain.
   The price is paid, Alleluia –
   amazing grace,
   so strong and sure!
   And so with all my heart,
   my life in every part,
   I live to thank you
   for the price you paid.

2 The price is paid: see Satan flee away –
   for Jesus, crucified, destroys his power.
   No more to pay! Let accusation cease:
   in Christ there is no condemnation now!
      The price is paid . . .

3 The price is paid: and by that scourging cruel,
   he took our sicknesses as if his own.
   And by his wounds, his body broken there,
   his healing touch may now by faith be known.
      The price is paid . . .

4 The price is paid: 'Worthy the Lamb!' we cry –
   eternity shall never cease his praise.
   The Church of Christ shall rule upon the earth:
   in Jesus' name we have authority!
      The price is paid . . .

207 Melody Green
© Birdwing Music / Cherry Lane Music

1 There is a Redeemer,
   Jesus, God's own Son,
   precious Lamb of God, Messiah,
   holy One.
      Thank you, O my Father,
      for giving us your Son,
      and leaving your Spirit
      till the work on earth is done.

2 Jesus, my Redeemer,
   name above all names,
   precious Son of God, Messiah,
   Lamb for sinners slain:
      Thank you . . .

3 When I stand in glory
   I will see his face,
   and there I'll serve my king for ever
   in that holy place.
      Thank you . . .

208 From Psalm 24
© Christopher Idle / Jubilate Hymns †

1 This earth belongs to God,
   the world, its wealth, and all its people;
   he formed the waters wide
   and fashioned every sea and shore.
      ᴬWho may go up the hill of the Lord
      and stand in the place of holiness?
      ᴮOnly the one whose heart is pure,
      whose hands and lips are clean.

2 Lift high your heads, you gates,
   rise up, you everlasting doors, as
   here now the king of glory
   enters into full command.
      ᴬWho is the king, this king of glory,
      where is the throne he comes to claim?
      ᴮChrist is the king, the Lord of glory,
      fresh from his victory.

3 Lift high your heads, you gates,
   and fling wide open the ancient doors, for
   here comes the king of glory
   taking universal power.
      ᴬWho is the king, this king of glory,
      what is the power by which he reigns?
      ᴮChrist is the king, his cross his glory,
      and by love he rules.

4 All glory be to God
   the Father, Son, and Holy Spirit;
   from ages past it was,
   is now, and evermore shall be.

(The singers may divide at A and B)

209 Dale Garratt
© 1970 Scripture in Song / Thankyou Music

Through our God we shall do valiantly –
it is he who will tread down our enemies;
we'll sing and shout his victory:
Christ is king!

For God has won the victory
and set his people free;
his word has slain the enemy,
the earth shall stand and see
that
   Through our God . . .

   Christ is king,
   Christ is king,
   Christ is king!

210 F .l van Alstyne (1820–1915)

1 To God be the glory!
      great things he has done;
   so loved he the world
      that he gave us his Son
   who yielded his life
      an atonement for sin,
   and opened the life-gate
      that all may go in.
   Praise the Lord, praise the Lord!
   let the earth hear his voice;
   praise the Lord, praise the Lord!
   let the people rejoice:
   O come to the Father
   through Jesus the Son
   and give him the glory –
   great things he has done.

2 O perfect redemption,
      the purchase of blood!
   to every believer
      the promise of God:
   the vilest offender
      who truly believes,
   that moment from Jesus
      a pardon receives.
   Praise the Lord . . .

3 Great things he has taught us,
     great things he has done,
and great our rejoicing
     through Jesus the Son:
but purer and higher and
     greater will be
our wonder, our gladness,
     when Jesus we see!
     Praise the Lord, praise the Lord!
     let the earth hear his voice;
     praise the Lord, praise the Lord!
     let the people rejoice:
     O come to the Father
     through Jesus the Son
     and give him the glory –
     great things he has done.

211
J E Seddon (1915–1983)
© Mrs M Seddon / Jubilate Hymns †

1 To him we come –
Jesus Christ our Lord,
God's own living Word,
his dear Son:
in him there is no east and west,
in him all nations shall be blessed;
to all he offers peace and rest –
     loving Lord!

2 In him we live –
Christ our strength and stay,
life and truth and way,
friend divine:
his power can break the chains of sin,
still all life's storms without, within,
help us the daily fight to win –
     living Lord!

3 For him we go –
soldiers of the cross,
counting all things loss
him to know:
going to every land and race,
preaching to all redeeming grace,
building his church in every place –
     conquering Lord!

4 With him we serve –
his the work we share
with saints everywhere,
near and far;
one in the task which faith requires,
one in the zeal which never tires,
one in the hope his love inspires –
     coming Lord!

5 Onward we go –
faithful, bold, and true,
called his will to do
day by day
till, at the last, with joy we'll see
Jesus, in glorious majesty;
live with him through eternity –
     reigning Lord!

212
From Jude 24 and 25
© in this version Word & Music /
Jubilate Hymns †

To him who is able to keep us from falling
and to present us before his glorious presence
without fault and with great joy –
to the only God our Saviour
be glory, majesty, power and authority,
through Jesus Christ our Lord,
before all ages,
now and for evermore! Amen.

213
© 1986 Trevor King / Thankyou Music

We are a people of power,
we are a people of praise;
we are a people of promise:
Jesus has risen –
he's conquered the grave!
Risen – yes – born again,
we walk in the power of his name;
power to be the sons of God,
     the sons of God
     the sons of God –
we are the sons, sons of God!

We are a people . . .

214
Graham Kendrick
© 1985 Thankyou Music

We are here to praise you,
lift our hearts and sing;
we are here to give you
the best that we can bring.

And it is our love
rising from our hearts –
everything within us cries:
'Abba, Father!'
Help us now to give you
pleasure and delight –
heart and mind and will that say:
'I love you, Lord!'

215
African origin edited by Anders Nyberg
© Wild Goose Publications /
The Iona Community

1 We are marching in the light of God,
we are marching in the light of God,
we are marching in the light of God,
we are marching in the light of God
     (the light of God).
     We are marching (marching;
          we are marching, marching) – Oh,
     we are marching in the light of God:
          (the light of God)
     we are marching (marching;
          we are marching, marching) – Oh,
     we are marching in the light of God!

OPTIONAL FURTHER VERSES:
2 We are living in the love of God . . .

3 We are moving in the power of God . . .

AFRICAN VERSE

1 *Siyahamb' ekukhanyeni 'kwenkhos,*
   siyahamb' ekukhanyeni 'kwenkhos,
   siyahamb' ekukhanyeni 'kwenkhos,
   siyahamb' ekukhanyeni 'kwenkhos
        (khanyeni kwenkhos).
     Siyahamba (hamba;
          siyahamba, hamba) – Oo,
     siyahamb' ekukhanyeni 'kwenkhos;
          (khanyeni kwenkhos)
     Siyahamba (hamba;
          siyahamba, hamba) – Oo,
     siyahamb' ekukhanyeni 'kwenkhos!

216
Malcolm du Plessis
© 1984 Thankyou Music

We declare your majesty,
we proclaim that your name is exalted;
for you reign magnificently,
rule victoriously
and your power is shown throughout the earth,
and we exclaim our God is mighty,
lift up your name for you are holy.
Sing it again, all honour and glory –
in adoration we bow before your throne!

217
Graham Kendrick
© 1988 Make Way Music / Thankyou Music

We shall stand,
with our feet on the Rock;
whatever men may say,
we'll lift your name up high –
and we shall walk
through the darkest night;
setting our faces like flint
we'll walk into the light!

1 Lord, you have chosen me
   for fruitfulness,
   to be transformed
   into your likeness:
   I'm going to fight on through
   till I see you face to face.
       We shall stand . . .

2 Lord as your witnesses
   you've appointed us,
   and with your Holy Spirit
   anointed us:
   and so I'll fight on through
   till I see you face to face.
       We shall stand . . .

218
© Michael Baughen / Jubilate Hymns †

1 We worship God in harmony
   with hearts in full accord;
   we share one Spirit, hope and faith,
   one Father and one Lord:
       In Jesus Christ our Lord and king,
       in Jesus Christ our Lord,
       the Spirit makes us all as one
       in Jesus Christ our Lord.

2 We're children now of God by grace –
   our new life has begun,
   where male and female, Greek and Jew,
   both bound and free are one.
       In Jesus Christ . . .

3 We live as those whom Christ has called
   to love with Christ-like mind
   that looks towards each other's needs,
   forbearing, patient, kind.
       In Jesus Christ . . .

4 One day we'll see him face to face,
   to him we'll bow the knee;
   we'll never say goodbye again –
   the best is yet to be!
       In Jesus Christ . . .

       (In Jesus Christ . . .)

219
Adrian Snell
© 1986 Word Music (UK)

1 We your people bow before you
   broken and ashamed;
   we have turned on your creation
   crushed the life you freely gave.

2 Lord, have mercy on your children
   weeping and in fear:
   for you are our God and saviour –
   Father in your love draw near.

3 Father, in this hour of danger
   we will turn to you:
   O forgive us, Lord, forgive us
   and our lives and faith renew.

4 Pour your Holy Spirit on us,
   set our hearts aflame:
   all shall see your power in the nations –
   may we bring glory to your name,
   may we bring glory to your name!

220
© Edward Burns

1 We have a gospel to proclaim,
   good news for all throughout the earth;
   the gospel of a saviour's name:
   we sing his glory, tell his worth.

2 Tell of his birth at Bethlehem,
   not in a royal house or hall
   but in a stable dark and dim:
   the Word made flesh, a light for all.

3 Tell of his death at Calvary,
   hated by those he came to save;
   in lonely suffering on the cross
   for all he loved, his life he gave.

4 Tell of that glorious Easter morn:
   empty the tomb, for he was free;
   he broke the power of death and hell
   that we might share his victory.

5 Tell of his reign at God's right hand,
   by all creation glorified;
   he sends his Spirit on his church
   to live for him, the Lamb who died.

6 Now we rejoice to name him king:
   Jesus is Lord of all the earth;
   this gospel-message we proclaim:
   we sing his glory, tell his worth.

221 I Watts (1674–1748)

1 When I survey the wondrous cross
   on which the prince of glory died,
   my richest gain I count as loss
   and pour contempt on all my pride.

2 Forbid it, Lord, that I should boast
   save in the cross of Christ my God:
   the very things that charm me most –
   I sacrifice them to his blood.

3 See from his head, his hands, his feet,
   sorrow and love flow mingled down:
   when did such love and sorrow meet
   or thorns compose so rich a crown?

4 Were the whole realm of nature mine,
   that were an offering far too small;
   love so amazing, so divine,
   demands my soul, my life, my all!

221A PRAISE SHOUT
From Psalm 107

LEADER Give thanks to God, for he is good;
ALL   **his love endures for ever.**

LEADER Let those whom the Lord has redeemed
        repeat these words of praise:
ALL   **O thank the Lord for his love
        and the wonderful things he has done!**

222 Wendy Craig
© 1987 Tembo Music Ltd

1 When I'm confused Lord, show me the way,
   show me, show me the way;
   baffled and bruised, Lord, show me the way,
   show me , show me the way.
       Still my heart and clear my mind,
       prepare my soul to hear
       your still, small voice, your word of truth:
       Peace be still! your Lord is near;
       always so close to show you the way,
       show you, show you the way.

2 When I'm afraid, Lord, show me the way,
   show me, show me the way;
   weak and dismayed, Lord, show me the way,
   show me, show me the way.
       Lift my spirit with your love,
       bring courage, calm and peace:
       you who bore all for my sake
       so I could walk from fear released –

with you beside me showing the way,
showing, showing the way,
showing, showing the way.

223 Unknown

1 What a mighty God we serve . . .

2 He created you and me . . .

3 He has all the power to save . . .

4 Let us praise the living God . . .

5 What a mighty God we serve . . .

224 Unknown
© copyright controlled

1 When the Spirit of the Lord
       is within my heart,
   I will sing as David sang;
   when the Spirit of the Lord
       is within my heart,
   I will sing as David sang:
       I will sing, I will sing:
       I will sing as David sang;
       I will sing, I will sing,
       I will sing as David sang.

2 When the Spirit of the Lord
       is within my heart,
   I will clap . . .

3 When the Spirit of the Lord
       is within my heart,
   I will dance . . .

4 When the Spirit of the Lord
       is within my heart,
   I will praise . . .

225 Graham Kendrick
© 1988 Make Way Music / Thankyou Music

1 Who can sound the depths of sorrow
   in the Father heart of God,
   for the children we've rejected,
   for the lives so deeply scarred?
   And each light that we've extinguished
   has brought darkness to our land:
       Upon our nation, upon our nation
       have mercy Lord!

2 We have scorned the truth you gave us,
   we have bowed to other lords,
   we have sacrificed the children
   on the altars of our gods.
   O let truth again shine on us,
   let your holy fear descend:
       Upon our nation, upon our nation
       have mercy Lord!

3 MEN
Who can stand before your anger;
who can face your piercing eyes?
for you love the weak and helpless,
and you hear the victims' cries.
ALL
Yes, you are a God of justice,
and your judgement surely comes:
    Upon our nation, upon our nation
    have mercy Lord!

4 WOMEN
Who will stand against the violence?
Who will comfort those who mourn?
In an age of cruel rejection,
who will build for love a home?
ALL
Come and shake us into action,
come and melt our hearts of stone:
    Upon your people, upon your people,
    have mercy Lord!

5 Who can sound the depths of mercy
in the Father heart of God?
For there is a Man of sorrows
who for sinners shed his blood.
He can heal the wounds of nations,
he can wash the guilty clean:
    Because of Jesus, because of Jesus
    have mercy Lord!

225A PRAISE SHOUT
From Psalm 80

LEADER Turn to us, almighty God;
ALL **look down from heaven and see!**

LEADER Renew us, O Lord God almighty;
ALL **show us your mercy**
        that we may be saved!

226
Mark Kinzer
© 1976, 1980 Word of God Music

Worthy, O worthy are you Lord,
worthy to be thanked and praised
and worshipped and adored;
worthy, O worthy are you Lord,
worthy to be thanked and praised
and worshipped and adored.

Singing alleluia, Lamb upon the throne,
we worship and adore you,
make your glory known.
Alleluia, glory to the King:
you're more than a conqueror,
you're Lord of everything!

227
Michael Card
© 1981 Whole Armor Publishing Inc. /
Cherry Pie Music

1 You are the Light of the world, O Lord,
and you make your servants shine:
so how can there be any darkness in me
if you are the light of the world?
    You are the light of the world!

2 You are the Bread of life, O Lord,
and broken to set us free:
so how can there be any hunger in me
if you are the Bread of life?
    You are the Bread of life!

3 You've overcome the world, O Lord
and given us victory:
so why should I fear when trouble is near,
if you've overcome the world?
    You've overcome the world!
So why should I fear . . .

You've overcome the world!

228
Unknown
© copyright controlled

1 SOLO Who is the Rock?
   ALL   The Rock is Jesus, the Rock.
   SOLO Who is the Rock?
   ALL   The Rock is Jesus, the Rock.

2 SOLO He blesses us:
   ALL   the Rock is Jesus, the Rock.
   SOLO He blesses us:
   ALL   the Rock is Jesus, the Rock.

3 SOLO He heals from sin:
   ALL   the Rock is Jesus, the Rock.
   SOLO He heals from sin:
   ALL   the Rock is Jesus, the Rock.

4 SOLO The Rock protects:
   ALL   the Rock is Jesus, the Rock.
   SOLO The Rock protects:
   ALL   the Rock is Jesus, the Rock.

5 SOLO He rescues us:
   ALL   the Rock is Jesus, the Rock.
   SOLO He rescues us:
   ALL   the Rock is Jesus, the Rock.

6 SOLO Who is the Rock . . .

7 SOLO Who is the Rock . . .

1 *Mwamba, Mwamba?*
Mwamba ni Jesu, Mwamba.
Mwamba, Mwamba?
Mwamba ni Jesu, Mwamba.

2 *Abariki:*
Mwamba ni Jesu, Mwamba.
Abariki:
Mwamba ni Jesu, Mwamba.

3 *Anaponya:*
Mwamba ni Jesu, Mwamba.
Anaponya:
Mwamba ni Jesu, Mwamba.

4 *Analinda:*
Mwamba ni Jesu, Mwamba.
Analinda:
Mwamba ni Jesu, Mwamba.

5 *Aokoa:*
Mwamba ni Jesu, Mwamba.
Aokoa:
Mwamba ni Jesu, Mwamba.

6 *Mwamba . . .*

7 *Mwamba . . .*

229
Eddie Espinosa
© 1982 Mercy Publishing / Thankyou Music

1 You are the mighty king,
the living Word;
master of everything –
you are the Lord.
    And we praise your name,
    and we praise your name.

2 You are almighty God,
saviour and Lord;
wonderful counsellor,
you are the Lord.
    And we praise your name,
    and we praise your name.

3 You are the Prince of peace,
Emmanuel;
Everlasting Father,
you are the Lord.
    And we love your name,
    and we love your name.

4 You are the mighty king,
the living Word;
master of everything,
you are the Lord.

230
Noël Richards
© 1985 Thankyou Music

You laid aside your majesty,
gave up everything for me,
suffered at the hands of those you had created;
you took all my guilt and shame,
when you died and rose again –
now today you reign in heaven
        and earth exalted.

I really want to worship you, my Lord;
you have won my heart and I am yours
for ever and ever:
I will love you.

You are the only one who died for me,
gave your life to set me free,
so I lift my voice to you
in adoration.

231
Mark Veasy and Paul Oakley
© 1986 Thankyou Music

You, O Lord, rich in mercy,
because of your great love;
you, O Lord, so loved us,
even when we were dead in our sins.

You made us alive together with Christ,
and raised us up (together with him),
and seated us (with him in heavenly places);
and raised us up (together with him),
and seated us (with him in heavenly places)
in Christ.

232
Amy Grant
© 1983 Bug and Bear Music / Kenwood Music

Your word is a lamp unto my feet
and a light unto my path;
your word is a lamp unto my feet
and a light unto my path.

1 When I feel afraid, think I've lost my way,
still you're there right beside me:
    and nothing will I fear
    as long as you are near.
Please be near me to the end.
    Your word . . .

2 I will not forget your love for me – and yet
my heart for ever is wandering:
    Jesus, be my guide
    and hold me to your side.
And I will love you to the end.
    Your word . . .

233
after E Budry (1854–1932)
R B Hoyle (1875–1939)
© World Student Christian Federation
and in this version Jubilate Hymns †

1 Yours be the glory! risen, conquering Son;
endless is the victory over death you won;
angels robed in splendour
        rolled the stone away,
kept the folded grave clothes
        where your body lay:
    Yours be the glory! risen, conquering Son;
    endless is the victory over death you won.

2 See! Jesus meets us, risen from the tomb,
lovingly he greets us, scatters fear and gloom;
let the church with gladness
        hymns of triumph sing!
for her Lord is living, death has lost its sting:
    Yours be the glory . . .

3 No more we doubt you, glorious prince of life:
what is life without you? aid us in our strife;
make us more than conquerors
        through your deathless love,
bring us safe through Jordan
        to your home above:
    Yours be the glory . . .

LEGAL INFORMATION

By the same Editors
in association with the Jubilate group

Carol Praise
The Dramatised Bible
The Wedding Book
Carols for Today

Church Family Worship
Hymns for Today's Church
Hymns for Today's Church: New Editions
Jesus Praise

Coming soon

Hymns 2000
Jubilate Hymns
Praise Today
Prayers for the People

Psalms For Today
Songs from the Psalms
Carol Praise for Children
Jubilate Versions

Jubilate agents in the USA

Hope Publishing Company
Carol Stream, Illinois 60188

INDEX TO BIBLE REFERENCES

Where Bible reference recorded

Amos
5.24 151

Micah
6.8 58

Malachi
3.2 172

Matthew
2.11 109
5.9 124
.13 63
.14 198
.44 148
6.9 33
.24 114
9.38 178
10.9 176
11.4 145, 194
.5 45, 56
12.50 133
16.18 84
18.14 6
20.28 40, 139
21.9 72
24.30 107
26.26 18, 133
27.29 221
.33 204
.45 91
.60 132
.62 122
28.2 233
.5 142
.6 43, 60, 132, 182
.19 41, 117, 142, 145,
      176

Mark
1.3 22
3.35 133
4.9 53
6.8 176
10.45 40, 139
11.9 72
13.26 59, 107
.35 59
14.22 18, 133
.36 1, 40
15.17 221
.22 204
.33 91
.46 132
16.6 60, 142, 182
.9 132
.15 46, 145, 196

Mark
16.20 220

Luke
1.46 170, 197
2.14 43
.32 112
4.18 51, 125, 164, 205
.19 126
7.22 45, 56, 145, 194
8.21 133
9.6 220
10.2 178
.4 176
.9 126
11.2 33
13.29 157
15.6 6
.13 80
17.21 66, 175
18.13 65, 101
.19 49
19.10 139
.38 72
21.28 109
22.14 133
.19 18
.26 148
23.33 204
.44 91
.53 132
24.6 142
.34 43, 60, 132, 182
.47 145

John
1.1 104
.4 229
.5 23, 112, 120
.9 227
.14 21, 220
3.7 144
.16 210
4.35 63, 178
6.35 5, 227
.48 5
9.25 6
10.16 173
12.13 72
.20 158
13.5 96
.34 133, 144
14.3 182
.6 69, 80
15.16 217
16.14 191
.33 227

John
19.2 221
.17 204
.30 56
.41 132
20.1 105
.14 142
.22 16
.24 233
.27 40

Acts
1.8 145, 217
2.42 146
4.12 80, 145
7.33 13
8.4 220
12.6 8
17.6 148

Romans
3.25 210
8.1 8, 86
.15 1, 30, 214
.17 199
.19 201
.23 156
.37 233
9.21 20
12.1 82, 193
.2 217
.9 188
15.5 218

1 Corinthians
2.2 221
6.20 204, 206
10.4 228
.16 56
11.23 133
.26 56
15.9 8
.20 132, 167
.55 173

2 Corinthians
3.18 120, 217
4.6 111
5.17 74
8.9 42
12.9 42, 169

Galatians
3.25 218
4.5 30
.6 1

PRAISE INDEX

WORSHIP INDEX

RESPONSE INDEX

INDEX TO HYMNS

INDEX TO COMMUNION SONGS AND HYMNS

INDEX TO PRAISE-SHOUTS

MAIN INDEX

*Italics indicate other names
by which the songs and hymns are known,
and also the Praise-Shouts.*